MUM

This was b[illegible] you with
all [illegible] 31st May
1991.

I hop[illegible]oy reading
it an[illegible] will always treasure
it.

Lots of love

Tracy.

x

xxxxxxxx

Ashmolean · Christie's handbooks

Worcester porcelain

1751 – 1783

The Marshall collection

Dinah Reynolds

Sponsored by
Christie's Fine Art Auctioneers
London

Phaidon · Christie's Limited
in association
with the Ashmolean Museum

To J. S. R.

First published 1989
Phaidon · Christie's Limited
Musterlin House, Jordan Hill Road, Oxford OX2 8DP

Published in association with the Ashmolean Museum

Published in paperback by the Ashmolean Museum, 1988

ISBN 0 7148 8062 0 (hardback)
0 907849 75 X (paperback)

A CIP record for this book is available from the British Library

Cover illustration: Miniature vase, Plate 4

Designed by Cole design unit, Reading
Set in Versailles by Meridian Phototypesetting Limited
Printed and bound in Great Britain by
Roundwood Press, Kineton, Warwickshire

The Marshall collection of Worcester porcelain

The Ashmolean Museum contains the most comprehensive representation anywhere of coloured Worcester porcelain of the 'First (Dr Wall) Period', 1751–1783. It was given in 1957 by Mr and Mrs H. R. Marshall in memory of their only child William Somerville, who had been killed in action in Holland, aged 21, in 1944. There are over one thousand pieces.

Henry Rissik Marshall (1891–1959), son of H. B. Marshall of Rachan, was educated at Marlborough and Trinity College, Oxford (where his son was also an undergraduate). He lived in London, becoming interested in Worcester porcelain in the 1920's, and President of the English Ceramic Circle from 1953 to 1957. In 1951 Mr Marshall arranged and catalogued the Worcester Porcelain Bicentenary Exhibition and in 1954 published *Coloured Worcester Porcelain of the First Period 1751–83*. He personally arranged the collection in the Marshall Room of the Museum as it had been in his own home, and classified it according to types of decoration. With only a few exceptions, such as the fine and exceedingly rare pair of blue and white candlesticks (Plate 11), the collection is entirely polychrome. For further information on Mr Marshall see *Apollo,* April 1983 'A Roomful of Crockery' by Ian Lowe, former Assistant Keeper, Ashmolean Museum, pp. 312–315; and *Ceramics,* May/June 1986 'Worcester in Oxford: Part One' by the same author, pp. 77–82. In 'Worcester in Oxford: Part Two' Simon Spero gives his reasons for the re-attribution of forty pieces in the collection to factories other than Worcester.

The Worcester Porcelain Company was founded by a deed of partnership signed on 4 June 1751 (now in the Dyson Perrins Museum, Worcester).

Among the original fifteen partners were Dr John Wall (649 bowl with part of the arms of Merton College, of which Dr Wall was elected a fellow in 1734), William Davis, the business partner (927 token money issued during a shortage of national coinage, 1770–80), and Josiah and Richard Holdship, whose rebus, an anchor, appears on some transfer-printed wares (617 and Plate 14). Dr Wall died in 1776 and William Davis in 1783, when the works were purchased by Thomas Flight. Under various owners production has continued until the present day.

Numbers throughout refer to pieces on display

In 1752 the Company took over the Bristol China Manufactory, started in 1749 by William Miller and Benjamin Lund, and acquired the right to mine soapstone (steatite) – which was used in the porcelain body throughout this period – near the Lizard in Cornwall. Many moulds were used both at Bristol and at Worcester, though 1040 is possibly Lund's Bristol as it has a tin glaze. The early period is well represented here with delicate painted decoration in Chinese 'famille rose' (746), 'famille verte' (Plate 8b), and Japanese Kakiemon (595, 601) styles. Shapes include the silver inspired sauceboats (853) and small creamboats (Plate 2 from a similar mould to the Wigornia marked piece at Worcester), the attractive pickle trays shaped as leaves (1013) or shells (1025), miniature jugs (588), small flaring Chinese shaped bowls (748, 752), and Chinese inspired vases (592). Among the tea wares are octagonal teapots (307, 309), tea-bowls and saucers (Plate 8b), rococo teapots and jugs (Plate 3a, 333), fluted bowls (751), four lobed cups (587, 591) unique to Worcester, and small ribbed cans (950). Favourite patterns are represented by Chinese ladies (Long Elizas) in gardens (309 and Plate 4b), 'famille rose' sprays (746), Chinese symbols (Plate 8b), and the Chinese stag hunt (Plate 3a), a decoration which continued in varying forms at Worcester for over twenty-five years. The Kakiemon style design of a long tailed bird perched on a rock (of which the 'Sir Joshua Reynolds pattern' is a version) was another favourite until the end of the Dr Wall period (608).

A group of wares from the mid-1750's with fine clean lines is known as the 'scratch cross family', from an incised 'X' or scratch mark which appears on the base of some pieces (599, 603). These included tankards with spreading bases and grooved loop handles kicking out at the lower end (1010) and distinctive bell-shaped mugs (Plate 6). Meissen influence on the decoration begins during this period, as seen in the tiny vignettes on double-handled sauceboats (79), and other pieces painted with European figures in landscapes or harbour scenes (80, 84 and Plate 5b), also, towards the end of the first decade, in the superb flower painting (750, 760), often executed in soft purple monochrome (97). The latter are frequently attributed to James Rogers, as are some of the naturalistic birds (Plate 9). There are pieces from this period with 'pencilled' decoration which often show Chinese influence (781–3).

By 1758–60 there were also bell-shaped mugs (297 with the 'Beckoning Chinaman pattern', 621), leaf dishes with landscapes (97), cabbage leaf jugs (Plate 9), which originated at Worcester, cos leaf sauceboats (743, 747), and the so-called 'Blind Earl pattern' (Plate 16a). Plates, production of which had been very limited during the earlier years, now multiplied (96, 99). The first experiments with ground colours began at this time with a soft yellow (663, 674, 680 and Plate 17b).

Armorial designs, the earliest of which date from 1754, were of particular interest to Mr Marshall. He acquired many examples of heraldic decoration (614–658, including Plate 6). They include some fine transfer printing by Robert Hancock (617, 627), who started working at Worcester circa 1756–7. With the exception of these, and a few other pieces (Plate 14), Hancock's work has scant representation here.

Moving into the next ten year period, shapes become more standardised and the colour of the porcelain body creamier. The durability and plasticity of the porcelain was largely responsible for the factory's success compared with Chelsea and Bow.

The wares show the perfecting of a fluted or barbed design (960), still produced and known today as the Warmstry flute, and a good circular teapot with plain (847 Kempthorne pattern) or flower finials (851). Oriental designs continued to be popular, especially the more elaborate Japanese Imari style, and include the fan (168) and old mosaic (728) patterns, and ho-ho birds (722). Sets of large vases were sometimes decorated with intricate patterns and shagreen borders (Plate 21). The 'famille rose' style continued but with Mandarin figures (302 with an unusual mask lip, 311, 336).

Continental shapes were introduced during the 1760's, for example the Meissen derived ogee form (Plate 32a) and squat cups with everted lips (769), which subsequently gave way to a more rounded cup (641). These pieces frequently have a mock Meissen mark.

The famous blue grounds of Worcester appear about 1765, and take the form of fish-scale (143, Plate 29), plain 'Mazarine' or wet blue (132, Plate 19), and powder blue (720, Plate 31a), where the pulverized cobalt was blown onto the moist biscuit porcelain through a tube, as was done in China during the Ming and Kangxi periods. Panels were left in these ground colours for painting later in enamels and usually with exotic pheasant-like birds (546, and Plate 31b), or bouquets of European flowers, inspired largely by Sèvres (554).

Two of the artists who decorated the blue ground pieces were Jefferyes Hamett O'Neale and John Donaldson. It is known that the former worked in Worcester from 1768 to 1770, but it is not clear whether Donaldson had the vases sent to him in London, as one authority states, or went to Worcester. O'Neale is probably best known for his Aesop Fable interpretations (117 and Plate 18) and other animal scenes (104, 106). Donaldson concentrated on figure subjects (103, 115, and Plate 19), some derived from classical legends.

Apart from the blue grounds which constituted the largest output, yellow, green, claret and turquoise grounds were produced, the green being the most popular after blue. Neither the yellow (659–94, and Plate 17b), nor the green (Plates 20a and 25a) grounds are gilded, which is so much a feature on the blue (Plate 31b) and claret (446 and Plate 20b).

From the late 1760's until about 1775, much Worcester porcelain was decorated in the London atelier of James Giles (1718–80), who advertised that he would decorate for customers in the styles of Meissen (419 and Plate 32a) and Sèvres (Plate 32b). In imitation of Meissen, Giles produced some elaborate overglaze scale grounds (73, 904, 925 and Plate 30b), a fine clear turquoise (Plate 33), a lovely rosy claret (440 the Hope Edwardes service, and Plate 20b), and a deep yellow (Plate 34) as well as yellow-scale (681 the Atherton service; 684 was, however, painted at the factory). The exotic bird painting from the Giles atelier (491, 516) was most distinctive and its boldly painted aggressive birds should be compared with those of the factory which often have background scenes (572). The very free flower painting in the same clear palette shows the influence of Meissen (Plate 32a) and Sèvres (1052). Other decoration includes naturalistic birds (490, 492 and Plate 28), landscapes in green (89 similar to the documented service at Corsham), and carmine monochrome (Plate 30a) in the manner of Tournai, and the rustic Teniers style figures (173), also Watteauesque children and lovers (Plate 31a). Many pieces decorated in London show Giles's distinctive rich, tooled gilding (573 and Plate 31b, versions of the Lady Mary Wortley Montagu pattern).

Attributions to Giles's atelier are made on the basis of similarities of decoration to that on pieces owned by his descendants (eg. Plate 29), or pieces made for people mentioned in his ledgers (629 John Martindale, 655 arms of the Duke of Portland, the Duchess being a customer). It is likely that the teapot (Plate 23) signed and dated 1772 by Fidèle Duvivier was decorated in London, whereas the Actor service (Plate 22) was possibly produced at the factory. Decoration in 'dry' blue was done both by the factory

(Plate 24) and by Giles (Plate 34) in imitation of Sèvres. Giles sometimes used different makes of porcelain when he decorated complete services (234 Worcester coffee cup with Chinese tea bowl and saucer) and also flawed pieces.

The painted decoration of the final phase of the Dr Wall period illustrates the marked change in style to the neo-classical, whilst shapes remained basically the same. One change in tea wares which should be noted is that the barbed flutes of the earlier period give way to rounded or reeded shapes (358, Plate 32b). Particularly attractive are the barrel shaped teapots (249, 858) accompanied by charming jugs with covers (823). The influence of Meissen was almost completely superseded by that of Sèvres, with delicate hop trellis patterns (72, and Plate 27a), and swags of flowers (12). While blue was still the most popular colour, it took on a lighter, brighter tone akin to the 'bleu de roi' of Sèvres, and it is used in a more restrained way with landscapes (Plate 26), fruit (14), and urns (44).

Worcester produced few items that were not purely functional except garnitures of vases (Plate 28), but amongst these were a few figures (883–9, 914–8), tubs of flowers (Plate 16b), and tureens shaped as partridges (Plate 13a) and cauliflowers (Plate 13b).

Marks: Many pieces are unmarked. Before 1760 sometimes there is a workman's mark (747, 766 and Plate 6), but otherwise they are rare. The crescent, taken possibly from the Warmstry arms (the factory was at Warmstry House), is used from *circa* 1760 on blue and white wares and slightly later on coloured pieces. It is usually in underglaze blue. The overglaze crescent mark can be blue (569 open crescent), gilt or iron red. This is invariably post-1770 and appears on the Duke of Gloucester service (Plate 25b, solid gilt crescent), Bishop Sumner, and late quail patterns (903, 959 open gilt crescents). The latter pattern often has an open iron red crescent instead (185).

The square mark, which is probably of Chinese

derivation, also dates from the 1760's. Towards the end, 'W' appears in script and invariably in underglaze blue (846), often in conjunction with patterns inspired by Japanese or Sèvres porcelain. The block letter 'W', also usually in blue, belongs to the 1760's and is frequently found on baskets (1009). 1048 has the rare printed 'W' mark. 734 is the only pattern to have both the crescent and the square mark, whilst 1012 is the only one with 'W' enclosed in a rectangle. The mock Meissen crossed swords, which sometimes have '9' or '91' between the points (801), are usually found on shapes derived from Meissen and decorated by Giles.

773 **Vase** circa 1752
of lobed baluster shape painted in 'famille verte' style with flowering plants and grasses, and on the reverse with a flying bird and insects.
The companion vase was sold by Mr Marshall, with other duplicates, at Sotheby's on 27 January 1953 and is illustrated by S. Spero, *Worcester Porcelain: The Klepser Collection,* no. 1.
Albert Amor, 1985, *The Sidders Collection,* illustrates a similar vase (no. 1) but decorated in the Japanese Kakiemon style.
This rare and important piece, with its shape derived from Kangxi porcelain, shows the early mastery of both paste and glaze, as well as of the decoration. The soft colours and the meandering outline of the plants enhance the baluster shape.
No. 777 is a larger vase of the same basic shape but with more pronounced ridges. It is decorated in 'famille verte' colours with flowering plants rising from rocks, and a ho-ho bird.

Height 19 cm. No mark.
H. R. Marshall, *Coloured Worcester Porcelain of the First Period,* Plate 3, no. 45.

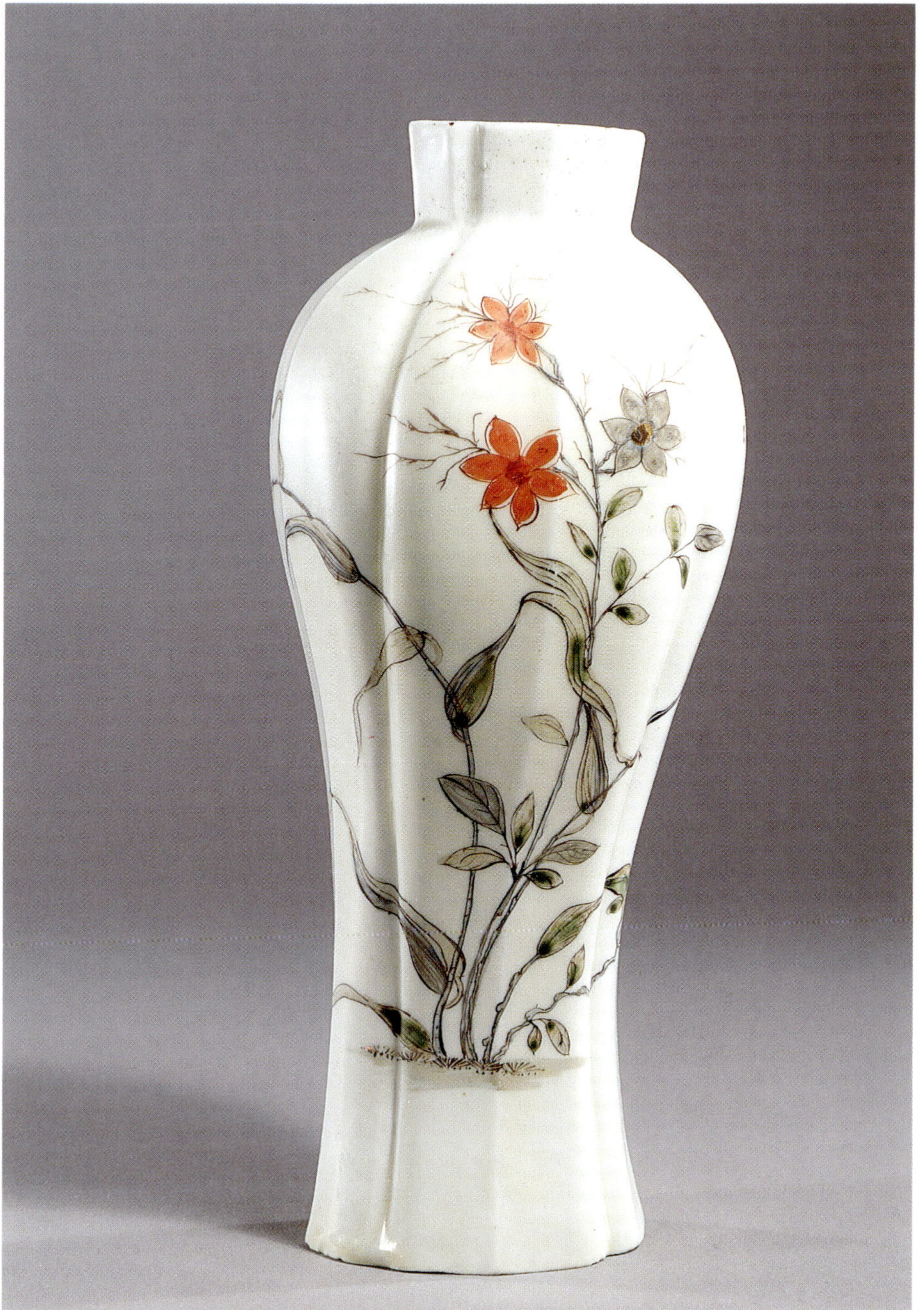

758 **Cream boat** 1752–55
of hexagonal shape with an angular handle. Moulded exterior of oriental buildings, fences, trees, birds and cattle in a continuous landscape, picked out in soft colours. Narrow inside border of green diaper and floral panels, and flowers in the base with a small leaf over a fire crack.
Similar in design to the famous cream boat now in the Dyson Perrins Museum, marked 'Wigornia' (the Roman name for Worcester) on the base. This type of cream boat has been separated into seven groups by S. M. Clarke of Chicago in a paper entitled 'Wigornia Type Cream Boats' in *The American Ceramic Circle Bulletin*, no. 3, 1980. To these has been added one more group by Dr Paul Riley in an, as yet, unpublished paper read to the English Ceramic Circle in 1987. This cream boat, with three others, has been entitled Type F.

Length 10.7 cm. No mark.
Marshall, *op. cit.*, Plate 25, no. 560.

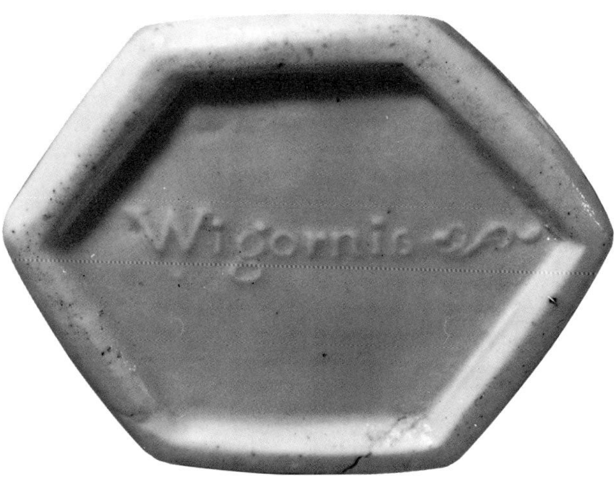

The Wigornia cream boat

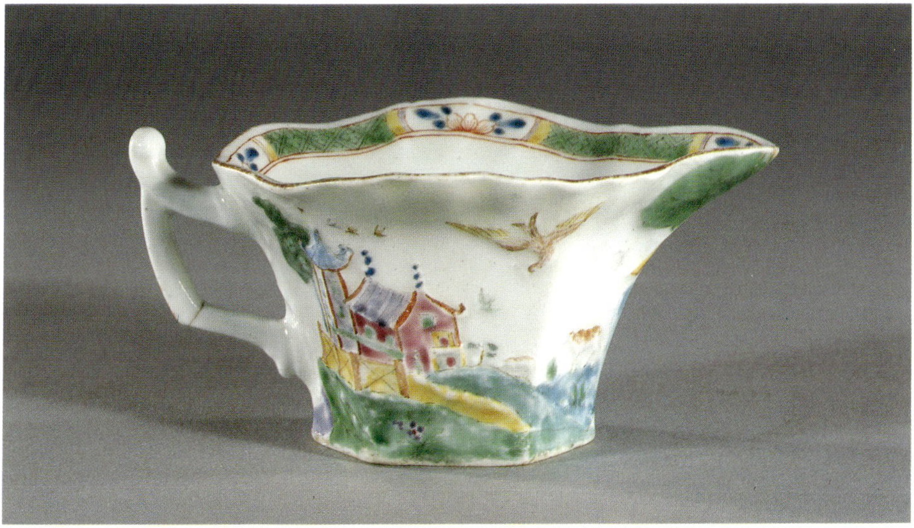

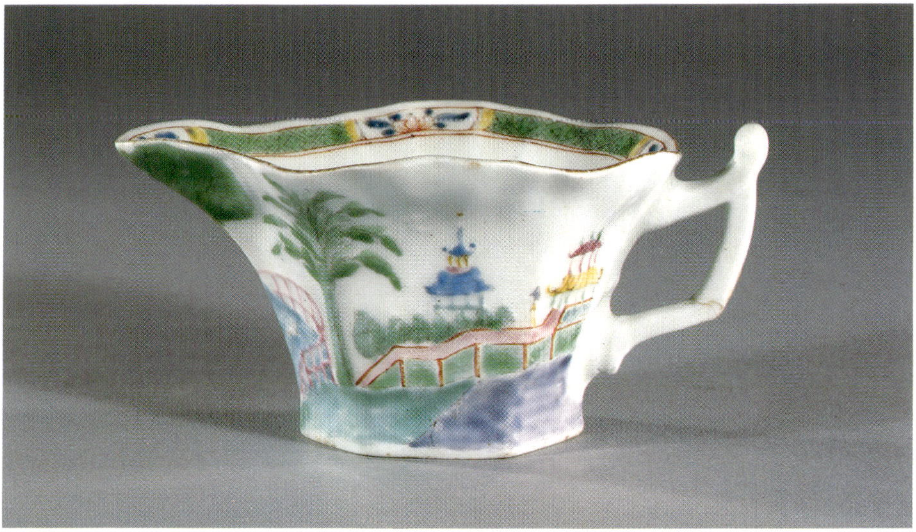

Plate 3

294 **Teapot** 1754–55
of moulded silver shape with sixteen pleats, and supported by four scroll feet. The lightly domed cover has a conical knop. Decorated on either side with a rococo scroll panel painted in soft colours with a Chinese hunting scene – the 'Stag Hunt pattern' – on one side, and on the other with two Chinese meeting in a landscape.
Exhibited Albert Amor, 1981, *Worcester Porcelain. The First Decade,* no. 24.
The 'Stag Hunt pattern', which first appears on Chinese porcelain (no. 209, see below), and possibly copied from a European engraving, was used at Worcester between 1754 and 1770, and was also used at Derby, Lowestoft, Chamberlain's Worcester, and Liverpool.

Height 13.1 cm. No mark.
Marshall, *op. cit.*, Plate 2, no. 25.

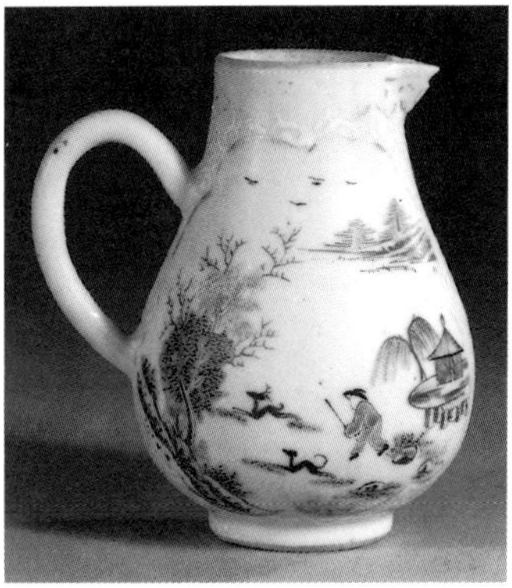

495 **Cream jug** circa 1754–55
with a moulded body and pear shape. The reserve on either side decorated in soft colours with an exotic bird among flowers. Double scroll handle.

Height 8.9 cm. Mark – moulded leaf spray, which is extremely unusual.
Marshall, *op. cit.*, Plate 25, no. 562.

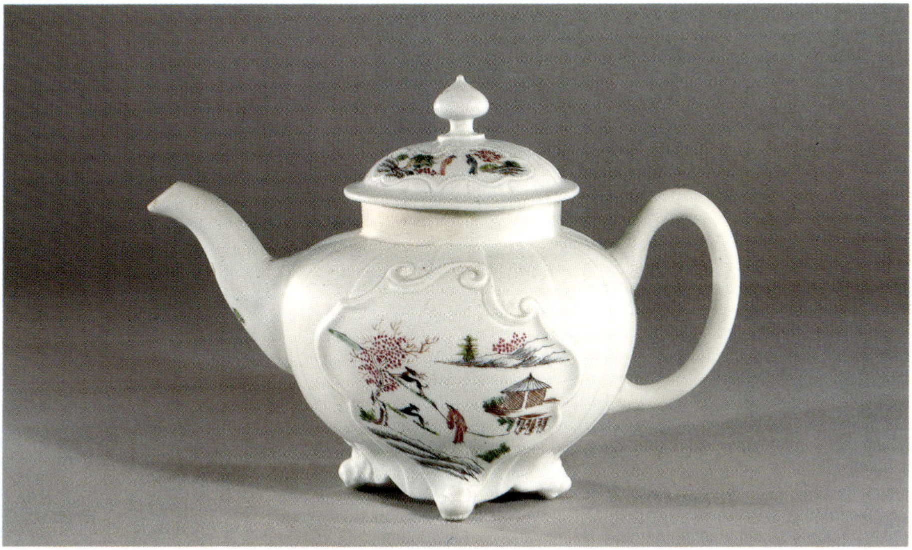

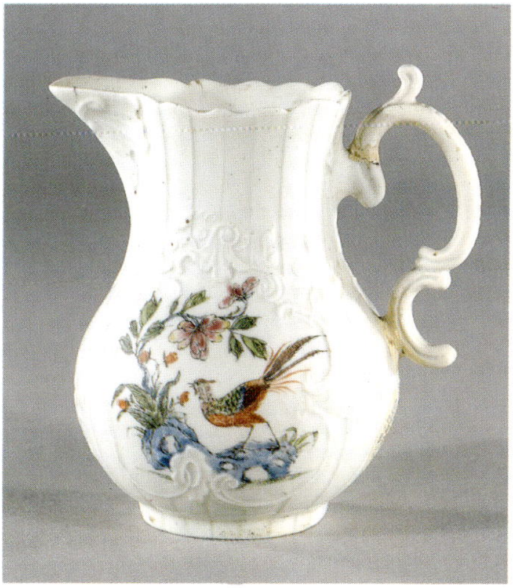

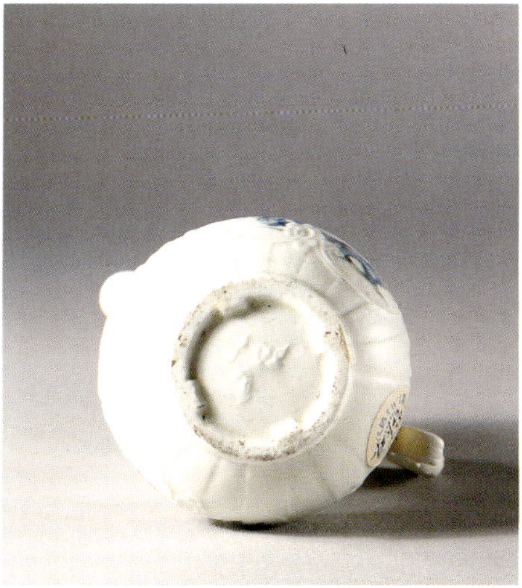

610 **Miniature vase** circa 1755
of hexagonal bottle shape, with a slender flaring neck. Painted in bright colours, on one side with a Chinese acrobat balancing on a table held by another Chinese, and on the other side with a landscape.
This shape of vase was the most common during the early and middle 1750's, and is used for a large variety of Japanese and Chinese style patterns, see nos. 609, 612 and 613. The acrobat scene is also found on opaque white glass which is attributed to South Staffordshire.

Height 10.5 cm. No mark.
Marshall, *op. cit.*, Plate 25, no. 573.
Similar exhibited Albert Amor, 1976, *Dr John Wall*, no. 2; and 1985, *op. cit.*, no. 8.

308 **Wine funnel** circa 1754
of trumpet shape. Painted in colours with a Chinese figure holding a fan, flanked by a pine tree and a plant. Inside border of green diaper and floral panels.
The shape is probably based on a silver original. There appear to have been three sizes of wine funnels made in the 1750's, of which this is one of the largest. Most have similar 'Long Eliza' (a corruption of the Dutch 'lange lijsen', slender ladies) decoration, which was also used on Dutch Delft.

Height 13 cm. No mark.
Marshall, *op. cit.*, Plate 2, no. 38.
Similar illustrated F. A. Barrett, *Worcester Porcelain and Lund's Bristol*, Plate 8a; and Spero, *op. cit.*, no. 31.

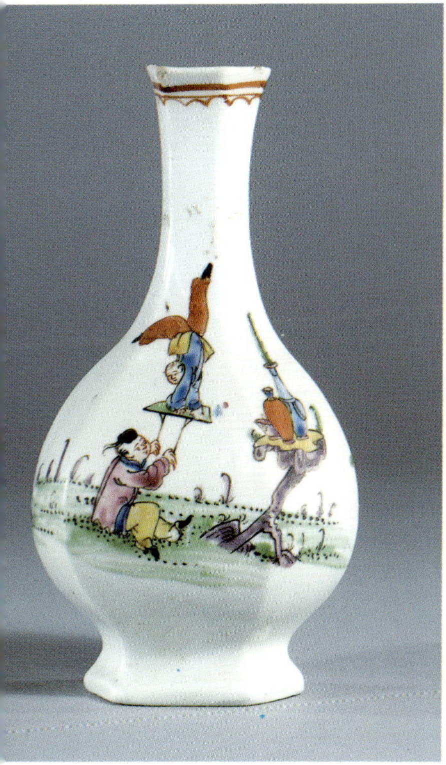

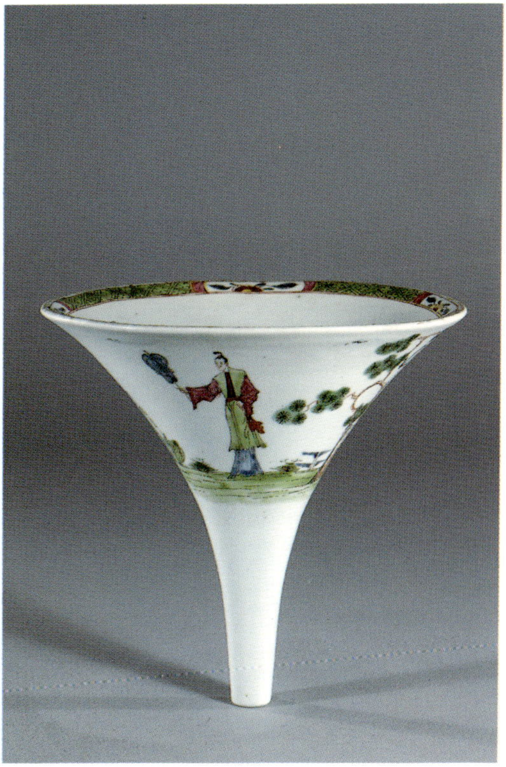

Plate 5

857 **Sauceboat** 1752–56

of moulded silver shape with oval pedestal foot and scroll handle, the thumb rest of which is coloured green. Decorated with moulded cornucopia swags picked out in colours, and purple ribbons. Inside border of oriental flowers and foliage, which are also on the base.

Sauceboats of the same shape, but with high scroll handles, are sometimes found with the mark 'Bristoll', though this one, and others like it, were probably made at Worcester during the 1750's. Dr Richard Pococke (later Bishop of Meath) wrote to his mother after visiting the Bristol factory on 2 November 1750, 'They make very beautiful white sauceboats adorned with reliefs of festoons which sell for 16sh. a pair'. (British Library, MSS Department. Cat. no. 15,800 Private letters.)

Length 22.2 cm. No mark.
Marshall, *op. cit.*, Plate 3, no. 52.
Similar illustrated Albert Amor, 1985, *op. cit.*, no. 6; and Spero, *op. cit.*, no. 23.

88 **Sauceboat** circa 1755

with crisp moulding on either side, of shells and rococo scroll panels picked out in pale pink and enclosing delicately painted European figures in a landscape (in the manner of Meissen). Under the long lip and around the scrolled handle are moulded prunus blossom and foliage picked out in colours.

Length 23 cm. No mark.
Marshall, *op. cit.*, Plate 3, no. 54.
Similar exhibited Albert Amor, 1976, *op. cit.*, no. 15.

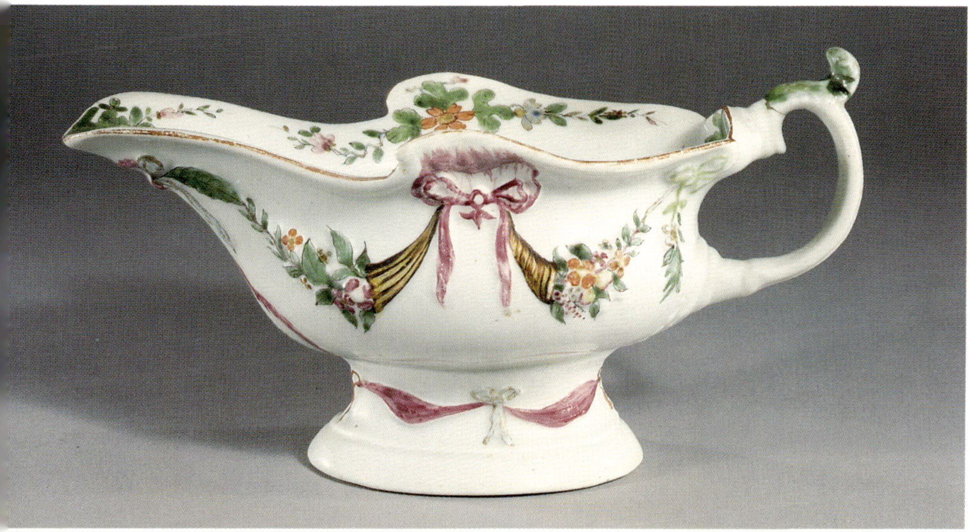

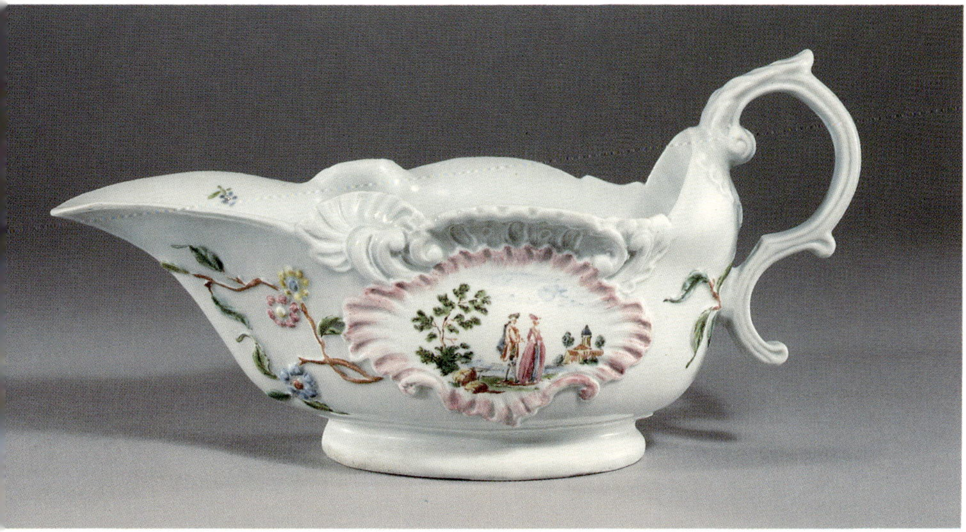

636 **Tankard** circa 1755
of bell shape with a grooved loop handle. Painted in colours and gilding with an achievement of arms, flanked by bouquets of European flowers. Coat of Arms – Quarterly 1st and 4th argent a chevron between 3 griffins' heads erased gules, Case; 2nd and 3rd azure a fess embattled or between 3 cocks' heads erased argent, Jesson; impaling or an eagle displayed sable, Weston.
Crest – A double headed eagle displayed or.
Motto – Virtus Vincit Invidiam.
This tankard is a good example of the 'scratch cross family', so called because many of the pieces have incised strokes or crosses on the bases. These pieces are usually thickly potted with fine clean lines and very little gilding. This tankard was probably made for Richard Case of Powick (1711–74), who was High Sherriff of Worcester in 1761, and whose mother was the daughter and heiress of Richard Jesson. There is a monument to Richard Case and his wife Ann, the daughter of Joseph Weston of Worcester, in Powick church, where Dr John Wall was baptised in 1708.
For this and other Worcester armorial pieces see article by H. R. Marshall in *English Ceramic Circle Transactions,* Volume 2 (1938–47), pp. 188–218, 'Armorial Worcester Porcelain'.

Height 11.9 cm. Mark – incised stroke on base.
Marshall, *op. cit.,* Plate 35, no. 748.
Barrett, *op. cit.,* page 21.
Pair exhibited Albert Amor, 1976, *op. cit.,* no. 18.

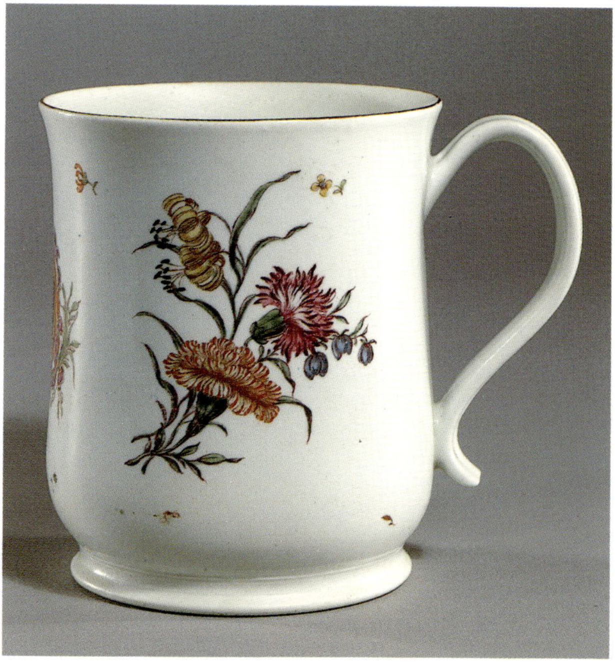

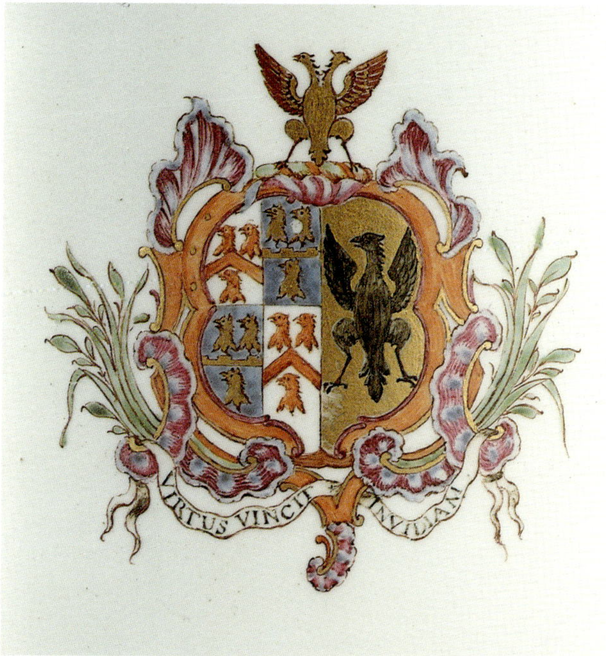
VIRTUS VINCIT INVIDIAM

Plate 7

920 **Dish** circa 1756–58
of moulded leaf shape with white serrated edge and short stalk handle. The central reserve is moulded with a scroll, and painted in soft colours with a seated shepherd playing a pipe, and two sheep. Surrounding the reserve are four bouquets of European flowers.

Length 19 cm. No mark.
Not illustrated in Marshall, *op. cit.*
Spero, *op. cit.*, no. 41, and no. 83 in *Transfer-printed Worcester Porcelain at Manchester City Art Gallery*, by E. Leary and P. Walton, are similar leaf dishes but the central panels are decorated with 'pencilled' figures. Albert Amor, 1981, *Worcester Porcelain The First Decade*, no. 57 shows the central panel decorated in a lilac-purple monochrome.

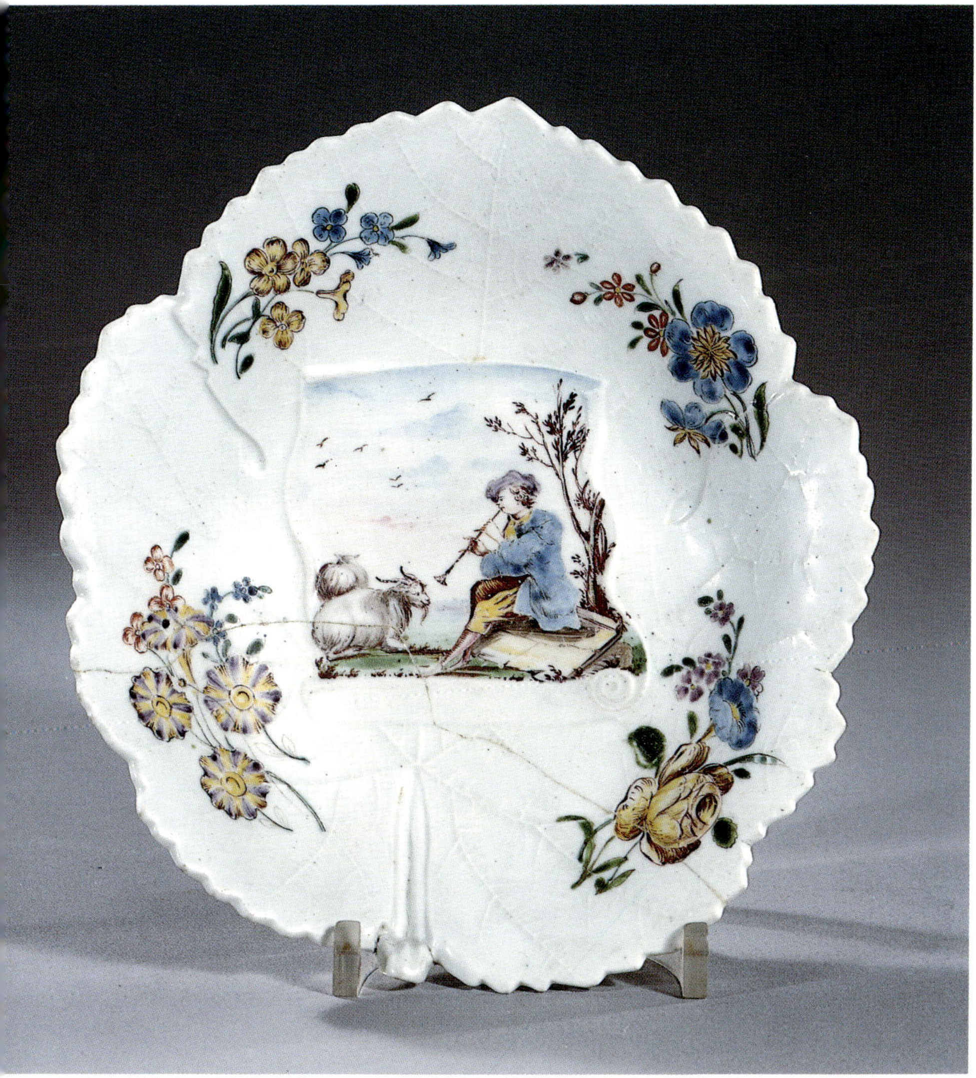

Plate 8

533 **Tea bowl and saucer** circa 1758
with ribbed moulding and a plain border. Decorated in Chinese 'famille rose' colours within a printed outline with a flowering peony plant on the left and two grey geese with pink fronts on the right.
This is an early use of a printed outline, and it is based on a Chinese design, of which no. 197, (see below), is an example. This decoration was also used on feather moulded and plain pieces, as no. 199.

Diameter of bowl 6.9 cm, of saucer 11.9 cm.
Marshall, *op. cit.*, Plate 22, no. 447.

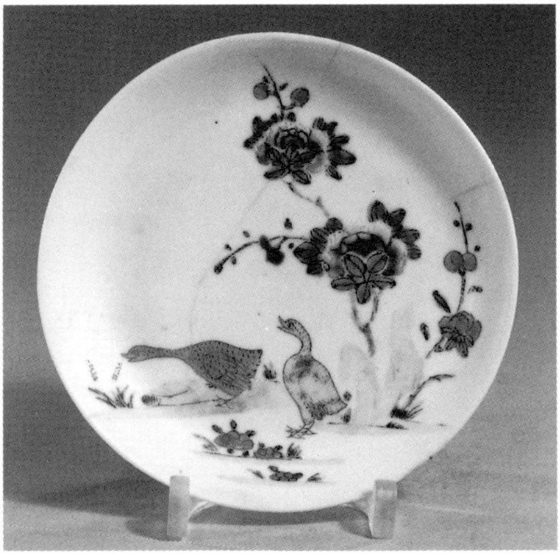

766 **Tea bowl and saucer** circa 1758
of octagonal shape, with Chinese 'famille verte' style decoration. Around outside of bowl and in saucer are alternate panels of flowering plants and garden ornaments. In centre of saucer and base of bowl are flowering plants within double red lines.

Diameter of bowl 7.1 cm, of saucer 10.8 cm. No mark.
Marshall, *op. cit.*, Plate 5, no. 83.
Similar exhibited Albert Amor, 1976, *op. cit.*, no. 27.

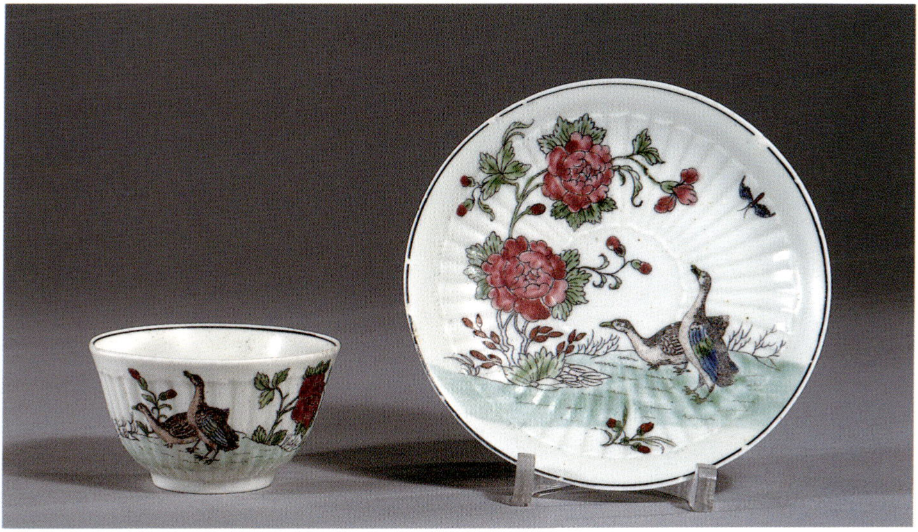

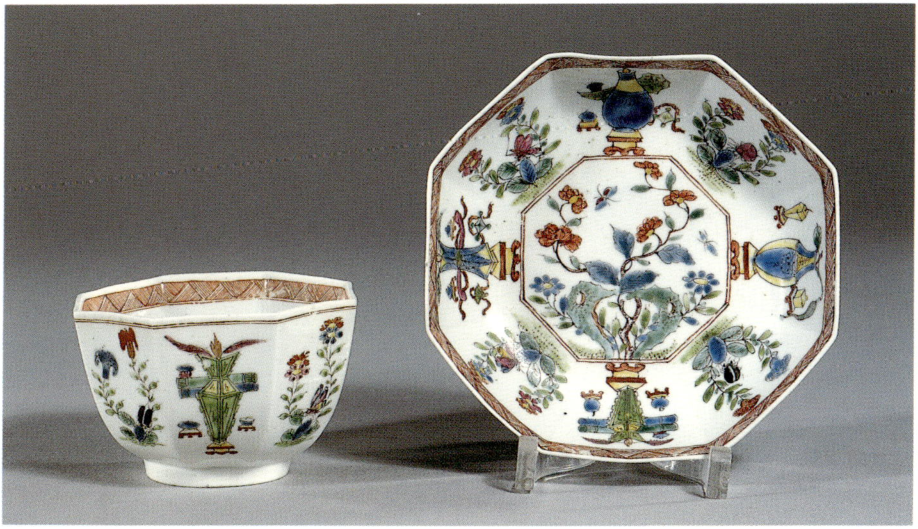

473 **Jug** 1758–60
of cabbage leaf moulded design with scroll handle. Painted in colours with European birds perched in a tree and on a fence, including an owl, pigeons and a pheasant in flight, all within a landscape, above crimson-pink rococo scrolling. Round the cylindrical collar of the jug is a narrow border of moulded green and yellow leaves.
This shape was produced throughout the Dr Wall period, but later examples usually have a mask lip spout, and were copied at other factories. Possibly painted by James Rogers, who was the principal enameller at the Worcester factory between about 1755 and 1765, and was probably responsible for the best work done at Worcester during that period. See article in the *Connoisseur,* April 1962, pp. 223–233, 'James Rogers. A leading porcelain painter at Worcester c. 1755–65'. In it Hugh Tait, of the British Museum, gives his reasons for attributing this and other bird painting to James Rogers, taking as a starting point the mug at the British Museum (see below) signed 'I Rogers Pinxit 1757'.

Height 20.2 cm. No mark.
Marshall, *op. cit.,* Plate 6, no. 109.
Exhibited Albert Amor, 1981, *op. cit.,* no. 69.
Similar jugs illustrated Barrett, *op. cit.,* Plate 15, and H. Sandon, *Worcester Porcelain 1751–1793,* Plate 26.

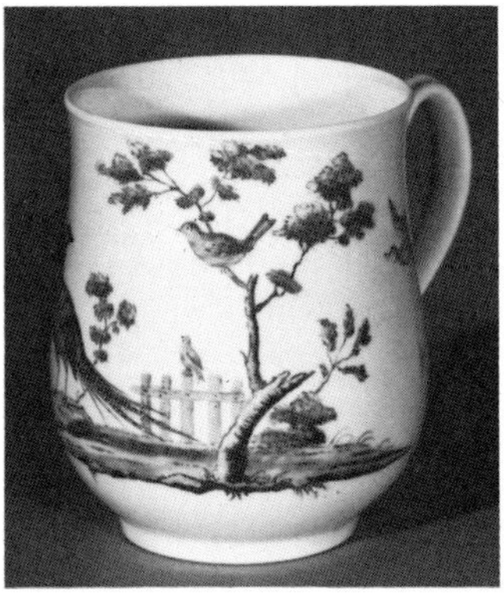

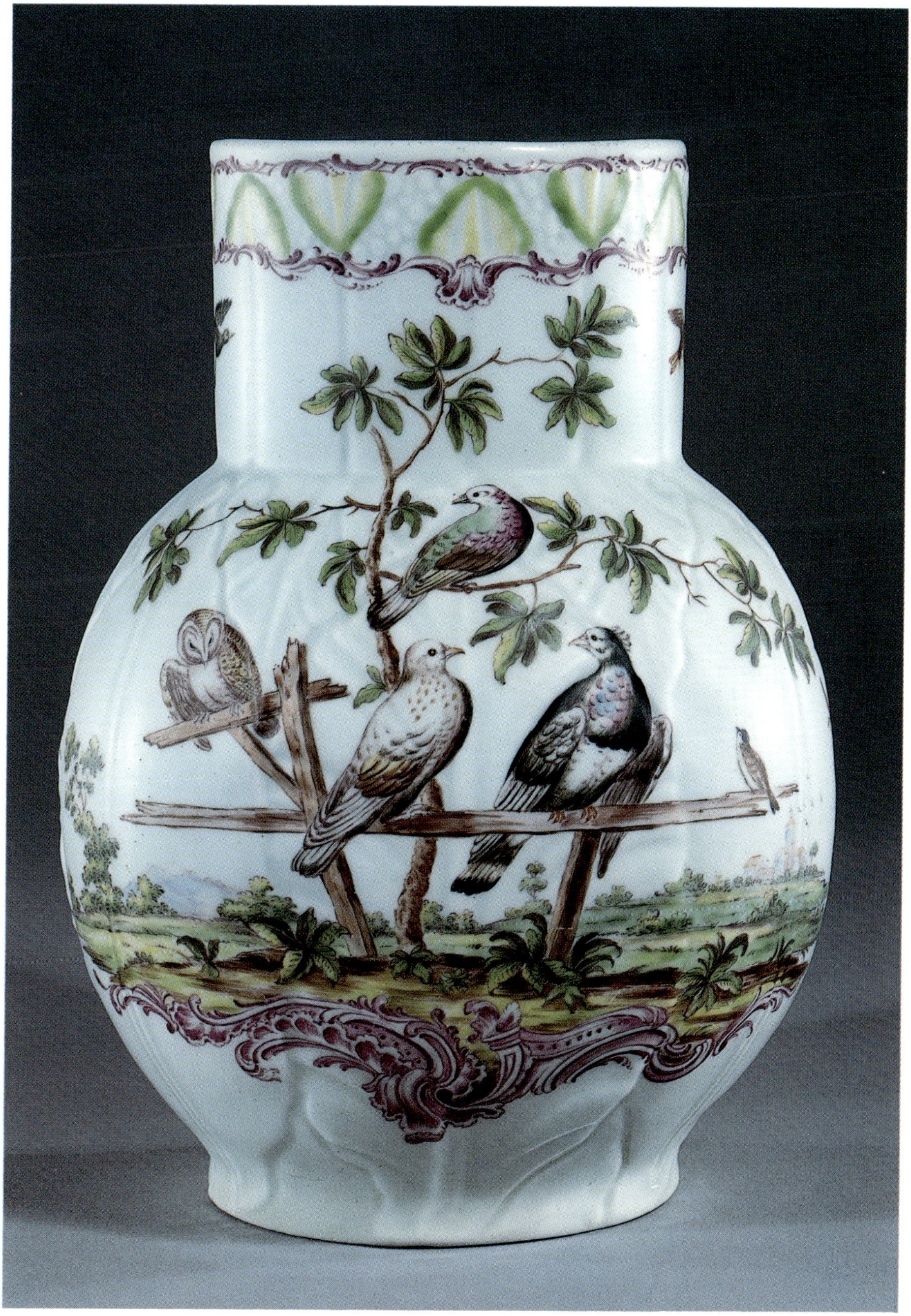

Plate 10

513 **Vase and cover** circa 1760
of baluster shape, with domed cover surmounted by a rose-bud finial. Painted in colours with a long eared owl perched on a branch with two other birds, and a host of mobbing birds. Bouquet of flowers on the other side.
This vase, probably made as part of a garniture, has (with nos. 93 and 402) been attributed to James Rogers.

Height 16.5 cm. No mark.
Marshall, *op. cit.*, Plate 32,. no. 701.
Similarly decorated vases and covers illustrated in Barrett, *op. cit.*, Plate 18; Spero, *op. cit.*, no. 53; Albert Amor, 1981, *op. cit.*, no. 70, and 1985, *op. cit.*, no. 21.

502 **Dish** 1758–60
moulded as a vine-leaf with a green branch handle. Painted in colours with a bee-eater bird perched on a leafy branch, and a butterfly.
No. 1068 has the same moulded shape, but it is painted more naturalistically with puce veining and green edging to the leaves, and three coloured insects.

Length 17.2 cm. No mark.
Marshall, *op. cit.*, Plate 32, no. 704.
Exhibited Albert Amor 1981, *op cit.*, no. 66.
Also exhibited at Albert Amor that year were a tea bowl and saucer transfer-printed in black by Robert Hancock with birds, including a similar bee-eater on the bowl.

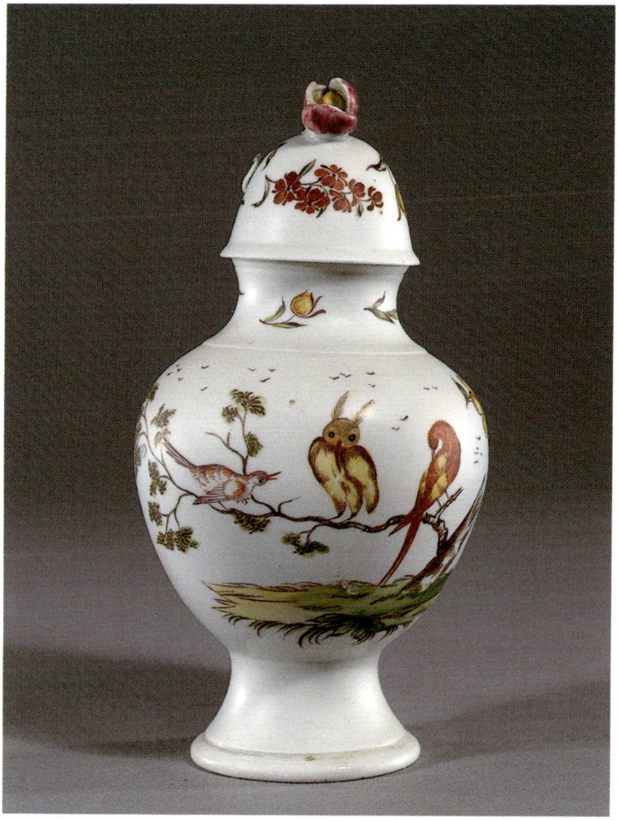

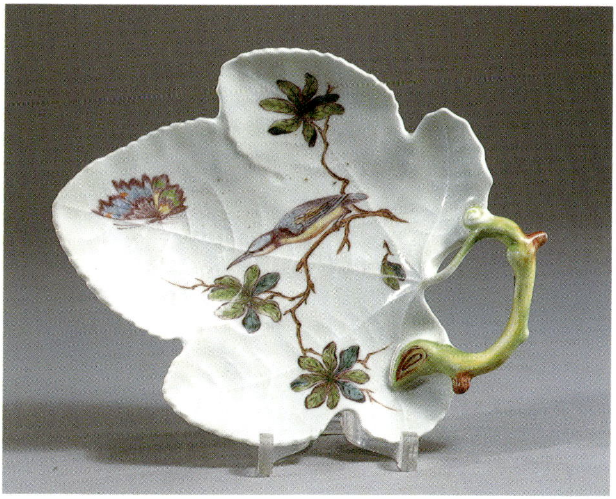

Plate 11

895 **Pair of candlesticks** 1758–60
both with circular base and gadroon moulding, and two ormolu joints between which is a moulded knop. At the top is a moulded nozzle. Decorated with underglaze blue flower sprays.
Though decorated in underglaze blue, which was not as a general rule collected by Mr Marshall, the extreme rarity of these candlesticks makes them an important adjunct to the polychrome pieces. The collection also contains an incomplete pair of polychrome candlesticks (nos. 878 and 882) with square bases, similar to the one illustrated in Barrett, *op. cit.*, Plate 21, now in the Dyson Perrins Museum.
Worcester also made chamber candlesticks, of which there are four in the collection. No. 879 has a satyr mask under the handle, a tulip shaped candle holder, and pierced rim and is decorated in 'dry' blue; no. 881 is similar but decorated in colours with bouquets of flowers; no. 568 is from the same mould but without the piercing and decorated with a scale blue ground and flowers in reserves. No. 924, however, has the saucer moulded as green edged leaves with purple veining, and a taller candleholder with detachable nozzle.

Height 24.1 cm. No marks.
Marshall, *op. cit.*, Plate 43, no. 888.
One exhibited Albert Amor, 1979, *Blue and White 18th Century Soft Paste Porcelain*, no. 59.

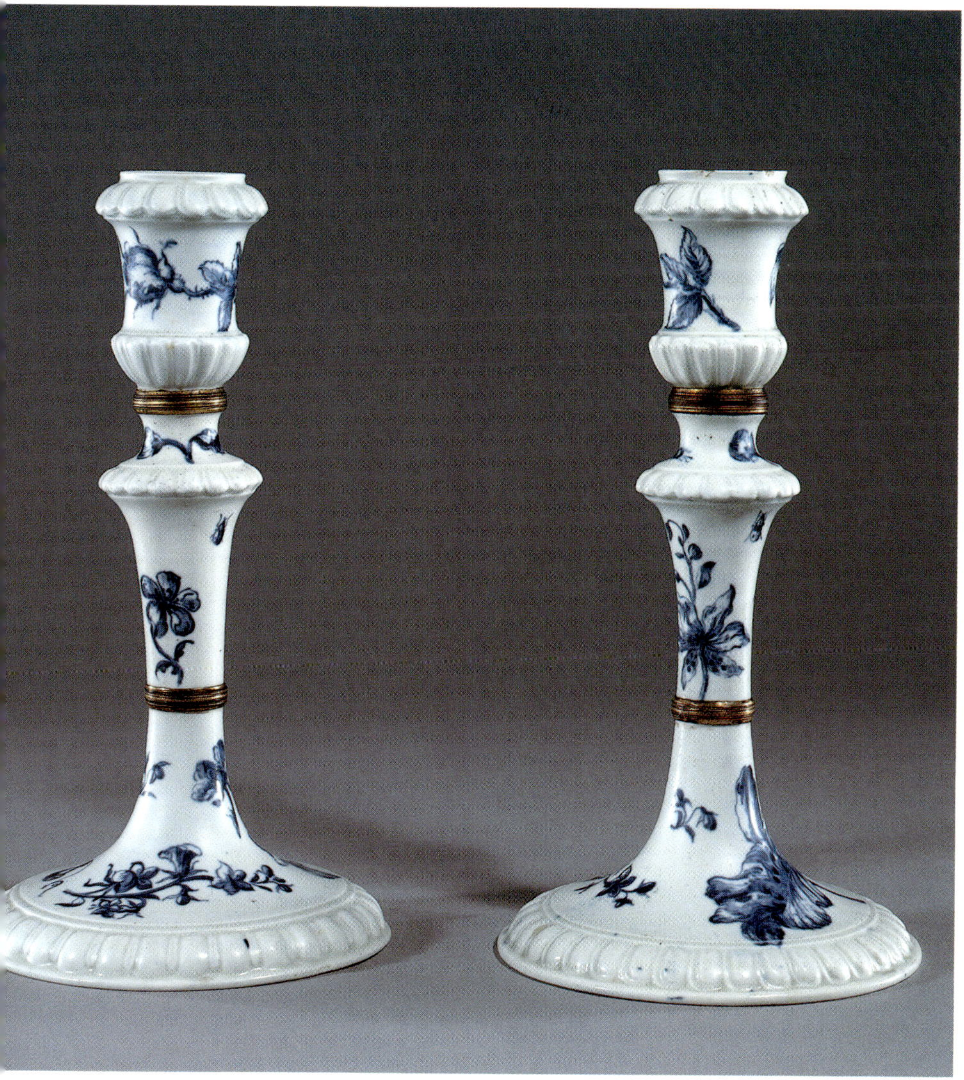

Plate 12

141 **Vase** 1758–60
of waisted cylindrical shape with a flared lip and spreading base. Decorated in colours with a gentleman and lady in contemporary European dress, and on the reverse with two birds on a tree by a fence and other birds in the sky.
The decoration on this vase was attributed to Jefferyes Hamett O'Neale by both Marshall, *op. cit.*, p. 43, and Barrett, *op. cit.*, p. 53. It must, however, be realised that the names of very few painters who worked at the Worcester factory are known. The birds on the reverse appear to have been copied from the same source as those on a vase in the British Museum (reproduced in colour in Hugh Tait's article on James Rogers, cited page 26) and are in the same grey and brick red, though less skilfully executed.

Height 14.5 cm. No mark.
Marshall, *op. cit.*, Colour Plate 15, and Plate 6, no. 94.

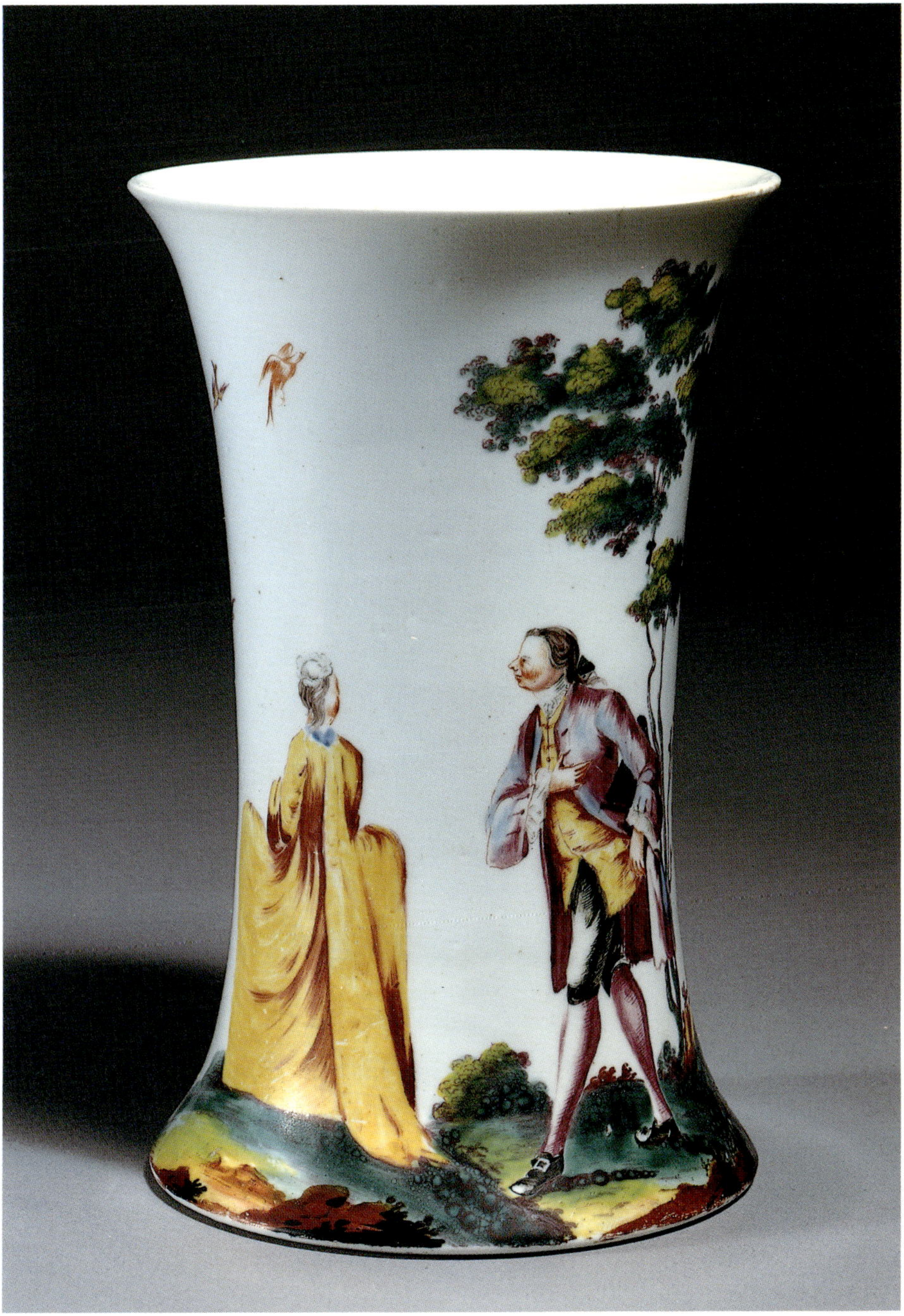

Plate 13

891 **Tureen and cover** 1760–65
shaped as a partridge sitting on a nest and painted in natural colours.
The pair to this tureen (no. 893) faces in the opposite direction. These tureens were copied from those made at Meissen, and were also made at Chelsea, Bow and Derby. No. 925 is a larger partridge tureen, left uncoloured. Such tureens are listed in an undated price card for the 'Worcester China Manufacture's' warehouse at London House, Aldersgate Street, London, opened in 1756.

Length 15.2 cm. No mark.
Marshall, *op. cit.*, Colour Plate 31, and Plate 21, no. 386.
Similar illustrated Barrett, *op. cit.*, Plate 87a, and Albert Amor, 1976. *op. cit.*, no. 82.

929 **Tureen, cover and stand** 1760–65
naturalistically moulded and coloured as a cauliflower. The stand is in the form of a leaf with stalk handle and has purple veining. Both the cover and tureen are decorated with two coloured and transfer-printed moths or butterflies, while the stand has three black printed butterflies. Unlike Chelsea, tureens modelled in the form of vegetables were uncommon at Worcester, and it is rare to find a cauliflower complete with its leaf.

Length of stand 21.2 cm, height of tureen and cover 11 cm. No marks.
Marshall, *op. cit.*, Plate 45, nos. 933 and 934.
Similar, without stand, illustrated Barrett, *op. cit.*, Plate 86a; Sandon, *op. cit.*, Plate 35; and with stand but without the transfer prints Albert Amor, 1976, *op. cit.*, no. 83.

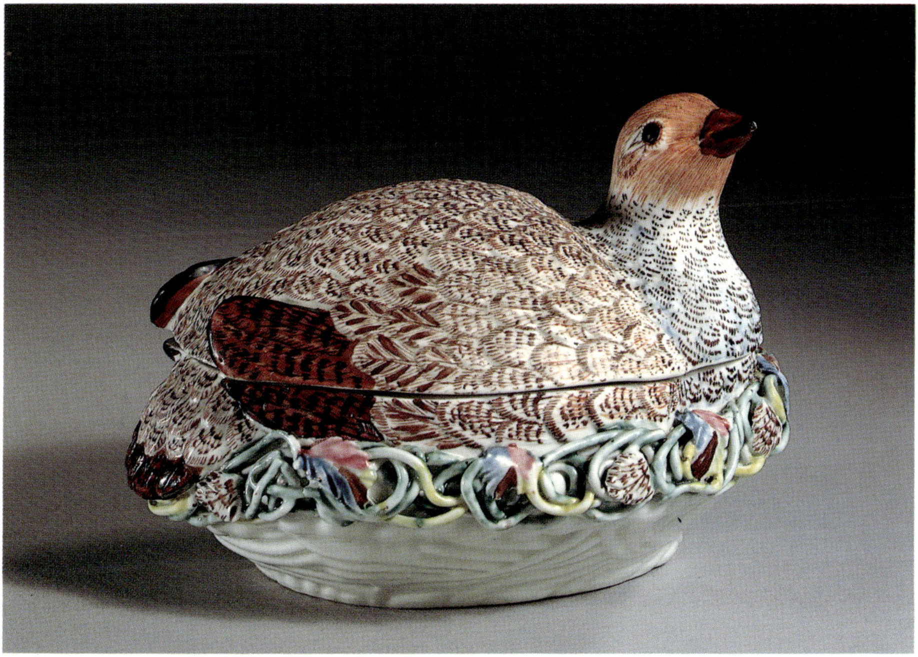

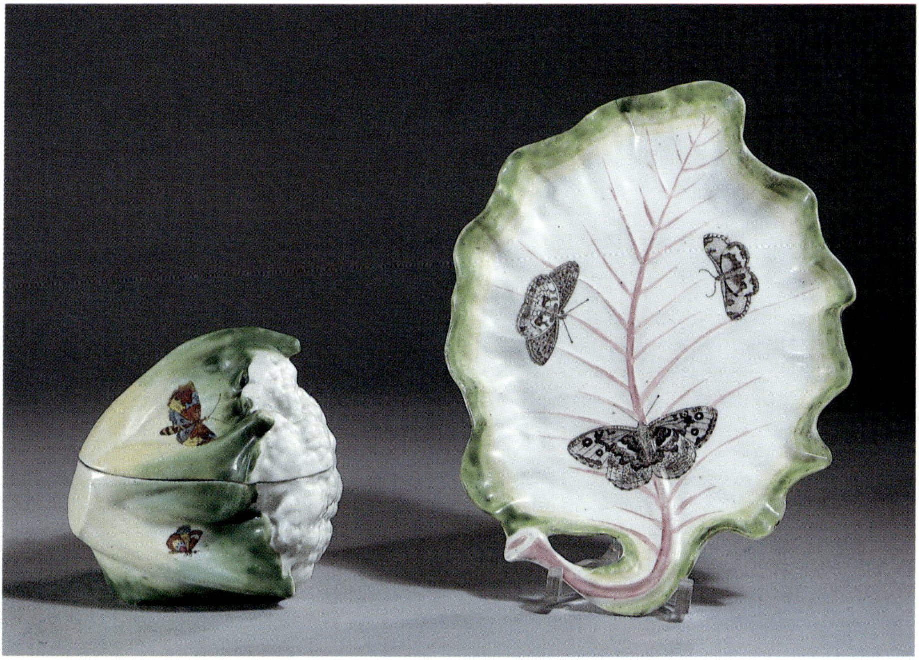

Plate 14

100 **Jug** 1760–65
of pear shape with scroll handle and mask lip, copied from Meissen. Transfer-printed in black and painted in colours, 'L'Amour' on one side signed 'R. H. Worcester' with an anchor, on the other side with 'The Tea Party'. These two scenes with 'The Milkmaids' are the most common of Robert Hancock's transfer-prints. 'L'Amour' is after a design by C. N. Cochin *fils* (1715–90), published by Vivares, and was first used at Bow. It can also be found on Chinese porcelain, creamware, Battersea and Staffordshire enamels and wall-paper. Hancock has added the Neptune fountain, garden roller and dog. 'The Tea Party', of which there are three main versions, was first used at Worcester between 1758 and 1760 and continued in use for nearly twenty years. The technique of transfer printing on ceramics was probably invented by John Brooks of Birmingham in 1753. He later became a partner at the Battersea Enamel Works where Hancock, before working briefly at Bow, could have worked under him. By 1757 Hancock was at Worcester where he perfected the technique, and later became a partner, but moved on to Caughley in 1774. For a full account of his life and work see Cyril Cook's *Life and Work of Robert Hancock* (1948), in which 'L'Amour' is Item 2, and 'The Tea Party' a variant of Item 105, no. 2; also his *Supplement* (1955); and two articles in the *Connoisseur* by G. W. Capell, December 1953, pp. 166–170, 'Some unrecorded or rare transfer printed pieces', November 1962, pp. 160–165, 'Rare porcelain decorated by Robert Hancock'. *English Transfer-Printed Pottery and Porcelain* (1981) by Cyril Williams-Wood, covers the history of over-glaze printing.

Height 18 cm. No mark.
Marshall, *op. cit.*, Plate 12, no. 215.
Leary and Walton, *op. cit.*, no. 35 has the same version of 'The Tea Party'.

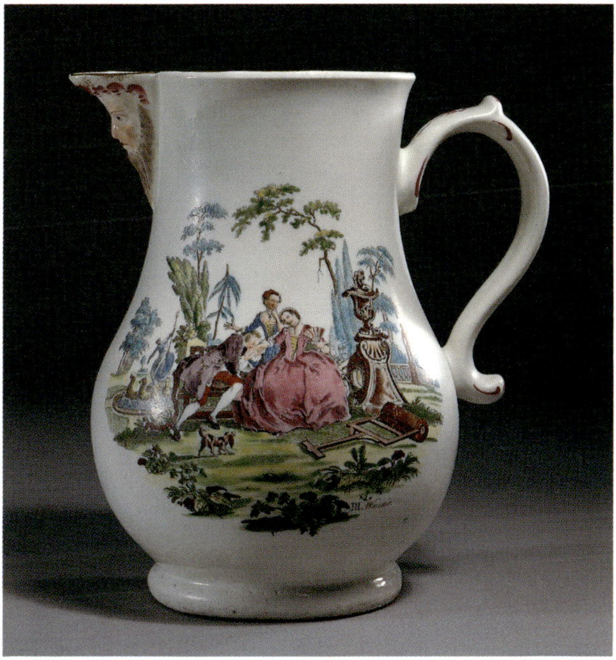

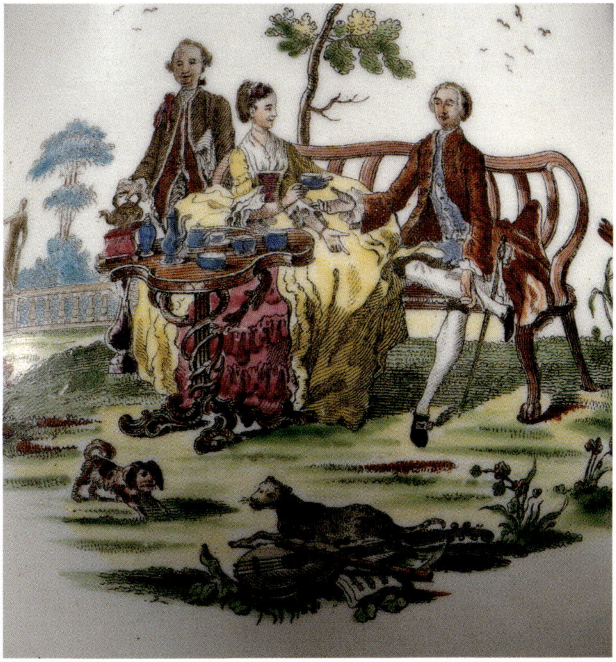

Plate 15

1030 **Cream boat** circa 1765
of shell moulded design, on an oval pedestal base. The shells are painted in shades of purple and yellow, and below the lip are two green and purple dolphins. The handle is modelled as a sucking lamphrey and also painted green and purple. There is a flower on the inner lip.
No. 1026 has the same moulding but is painted in different colours. These 'Dolphin Ewers', as they were called in the 18th century, were made in a larger size, and also at several other factories.
Lamphreys are eel-like fishes which live in the sea, but travel up rivers in the spring, and were considered a great delicacy, especially those from the River Severn.

Length 8.6 cm. No mark.
Marshall, *op. cit.*, Plate 50, no. 1015.
Similar illustrated Spero, *op. cit.*, no. 69, and Albert Amor, 1976, *op. cit.*, no. 43.

886 **Salt cellar** 1765–70
moulded as a scallop shell supported by a white rockwork base, encrusted with shells, coral and seaweed painted in vivid colours. The interior of the shell painted with flowers within a pink border.
No. 922 is a sweetmeat stand composed of four shells with rockwork joining the top shell to the lower three. It is decorated with the same bright colours as this salt cellar.

Length 10.2 cm. No mark.
Marshall, *op. cit.*, Plate 21, no. 389.
Similar illustrated Spero, *op. cit.*, no. 68, with the interior painted with exotic birds; and Albert Amor, 1985, *op. cit.*, no. 30, with flowers and more restrained decoration.

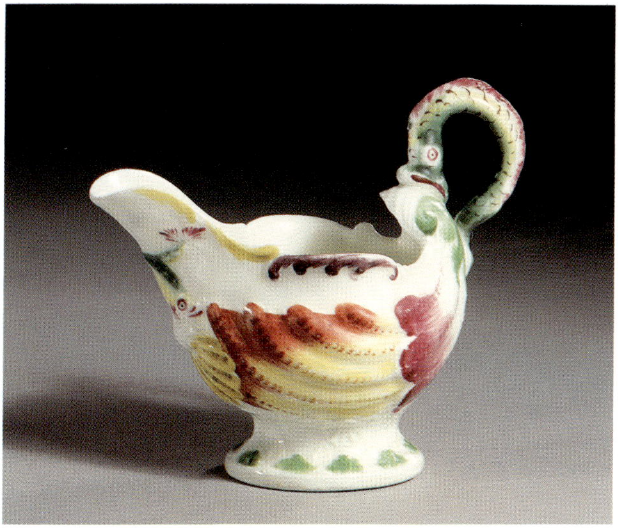

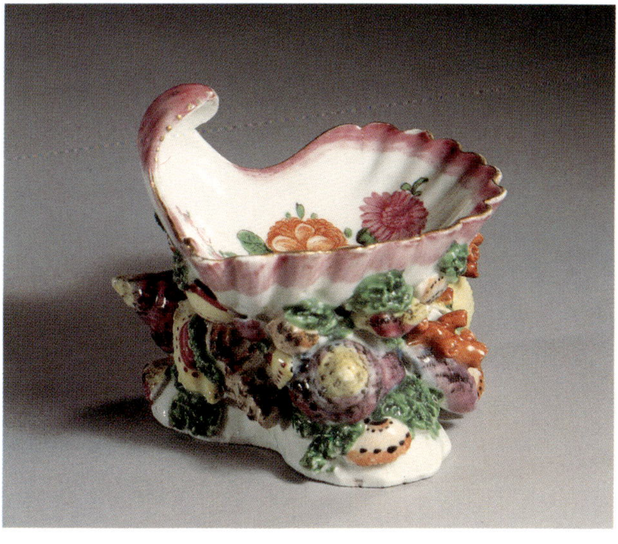

431 **Sweetmeat dish** circa 1760
with a scalloped rim and twig handle, and moulded spray of rosebuds and leaves picked out in natural colours – the 'Blind Earl pattern'.
This moulded pattern is traditionally associated with the 6th Earl of Coventry (whose first wife was the famous beauty, Maria Gunning), but who was not blinded, in a hunting accident, until 1780. It is rare to find an example such as this without any additional decoration. Many pieces have decoration which ignores the moulding, such as nos. 429, 446, 860 and 1011. Nos. 1054 and 1055 are larger versions but without the twig handle.

Length 16 cm. No mark.
Marshall, *op. cit.*, Plate 28, no. 609.

923 **Pot of flowers** circa 1765
made in two sections. Bucket shaped pot with two moulded bands, from the upper one of which depend three moulded gilt rings with coloured flowers between. The moulded petal rim is painted in colours. The conical encrusted floral bouquet consists of six garden flowers surmounted by cream may flowers.
There is another pot, but without flowers, in the collection, no. 1042. These rare items, which vary in decoration though not in shape, probably copy Vincennes or Mennecy.

Height 14 cm. No mark.
Marshall, *op. cit.*, Colour Plate 22, and Plate 20, no. 383.
Similar illustrated Spero, *op. cit.*, no. 70; and Albert Amor, 1976, *op. cit.*, no. 72.

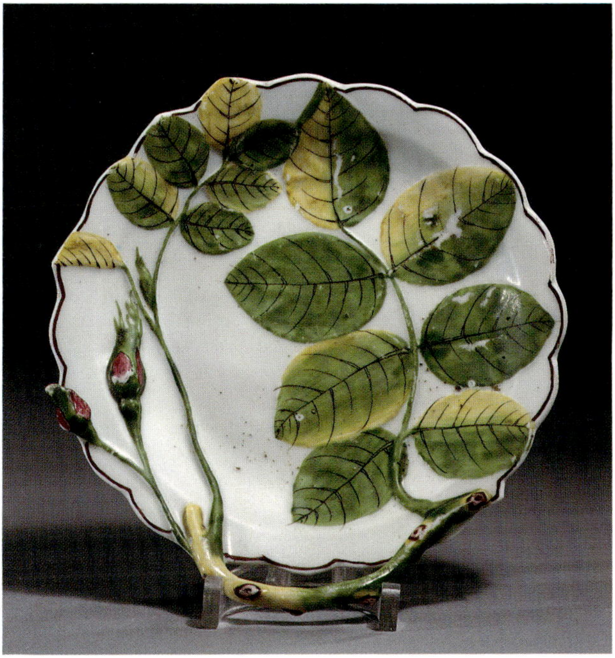

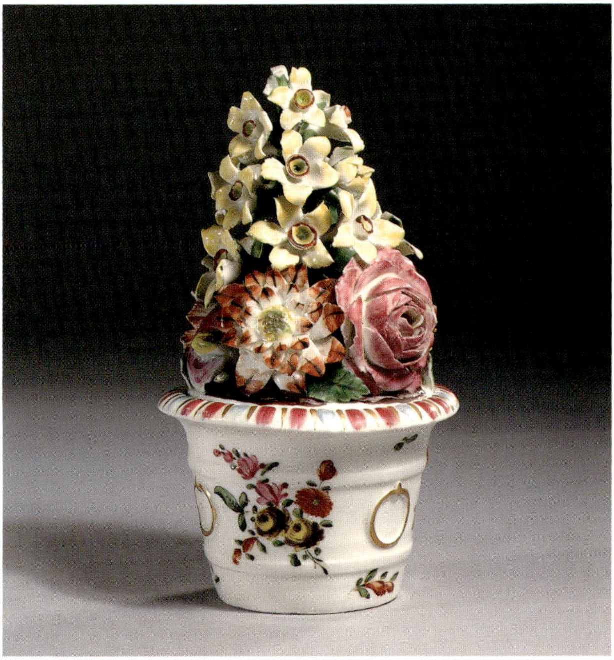

Plate 17

684 **Chocolate cup and saucer** 1765–70
of ogee shape, with solid scroll handles to the cup. The yellow scale ground is decorated with large rococo, gilt scroll bordered reserves painted in colours with exotic birds, and smaller reserves with insects.
The yellow scale decoration, possibly derived from Meissen, is rarer than the solid yellow ground and only seen with exotic birds. The leaves on the cup are painted differently from those on the saucer, as is also the case with a similar cup and saucer, but with pierced handles, exhibited Albert Amor, 1985, *op. cit.*, no. 52, sold by Mr Marshall at Sotheby's in 1953.

Diameter of cup 9.2 cm, of saucer 14.9 cm. No mark.
Marshall, *op. cit.*, Plate 30, no. 666.

686 **Dish** circa 1760
of oval shape, with four panels of moulded basket work, coloured pale yellow, alternating with four panels of pierced lattice work picked out in rust brown. Painted in colours with scattered sprays of European flowers and foliage.
There are four of these unusual dishes in the collection, all decorated differently, though nos. 685 and 690 also have flowers, but only in the middle, whereas the centre of no. 682 is decorated with exotic birds.

Length 26.4 cm. No mark.
Marshall, *op. cit.*, Plate 29, no. 644.
Similar exhibited Albert Amor, 1976, *op. cit.*, no. 20.

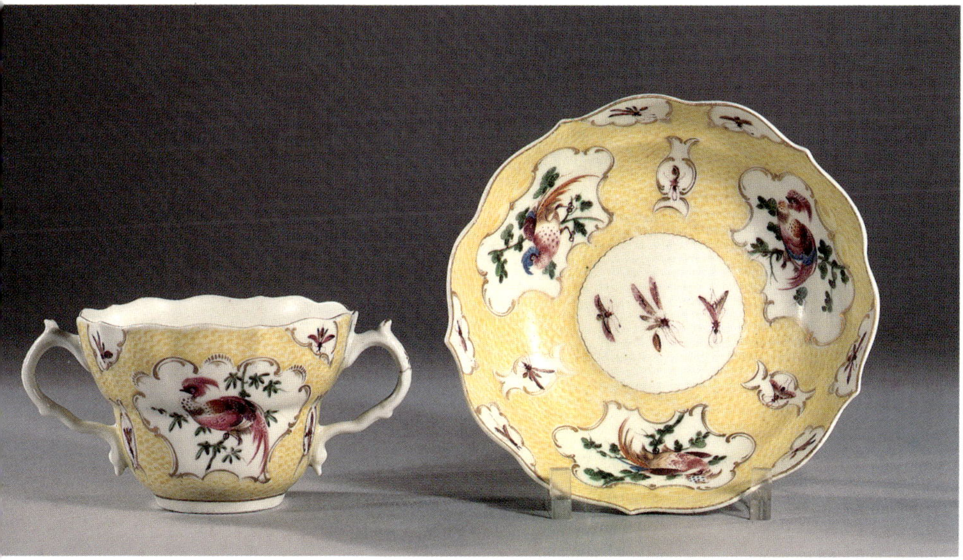

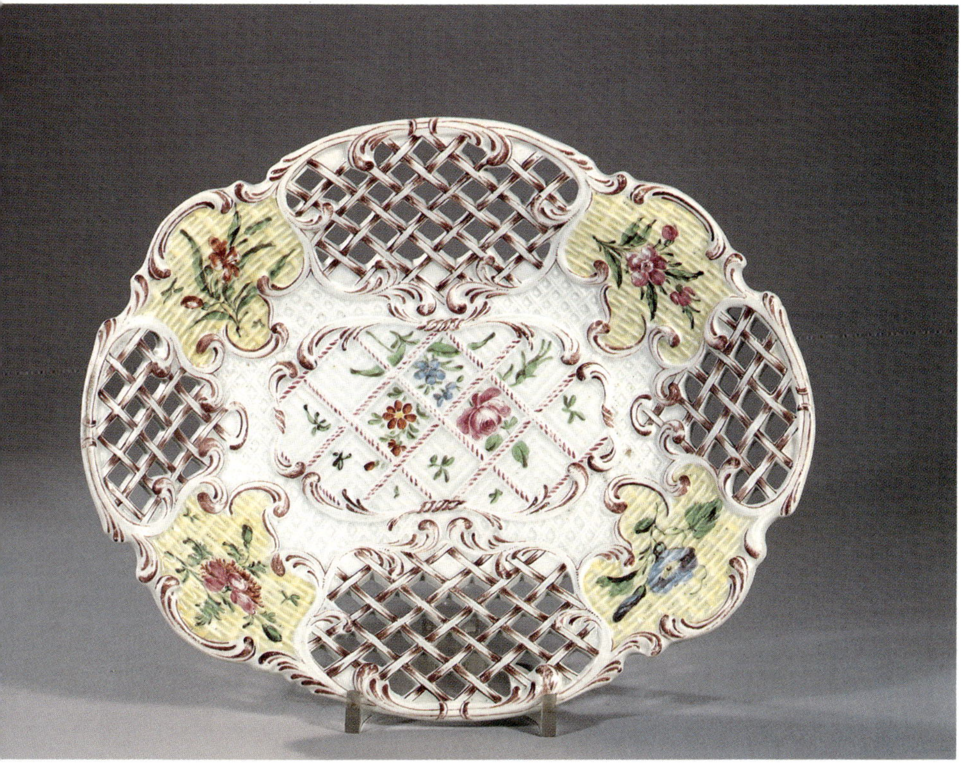

Plate 18

105 **Plate** 1768–70
with scalloped rim and blue scale ground. The central circular reserve is decorated with a scene from Aesop's fable 'The Ass and the Little Dog'. On the rim are four large irregular reserves, two with animals and two with exotic birds, and also four smaller triangular reserves with flowers.
This plate was painted by Jefferyes Hamett O'Neale (b. 1734, Co. Antrim, d. 1801), the principal fable and myth painter at Chelsea *circa* 1751 to 1758. He exhibited at the Society of Artists 1763 to 1766, and worked in Worcester from 1768 to 1770, but returned to work at Chelsea from 1771 to 1773. His work is found on early red anchor and late gold anchor Chelsea, Battersea enamels, oriental porcelain, Wedgewood and Derby, as well as on Worcester. Distinctive O'Neale features, which appear on this plate, include the brown rocks in the foreground, the blue hill, the overhanging eave, and the spotted cows and other animals in the smaller panels. In this fable the ass, who is often beaten, sees his master fondling his lap dog, so thinks that if he also gets onto his master's lap, he too will be caressed. This plate shows him attempting to do so, which leads to another beating.
Other pieces by O'Neale are nos. 117, 121, 132 and 136 – plates with fable scenes; 124 and 130 – lozenge dishes with fable scenes; 145 – large plate with fable scene; 104 and 106 – pair of vases with animals, of which the former is signed 'O'Neale/pinx' on the rocks; and 107 – ormolu mounted vase with 'The Trial of the Fox'.
Marshall, *op. cit.*, pp. 43–59, discusses the fable plates. See also *Jefferyes Hamett O'Neale* (1938), by W. H. Tapp.

Diameter 29.7 cm. Mark – fretted square.
Marshall, *op. cit.*, Colour Plate 12, Plate 27, no. 601.

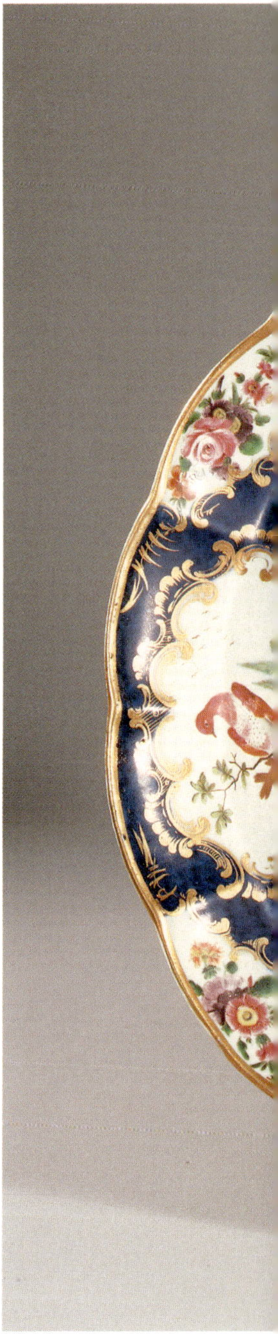

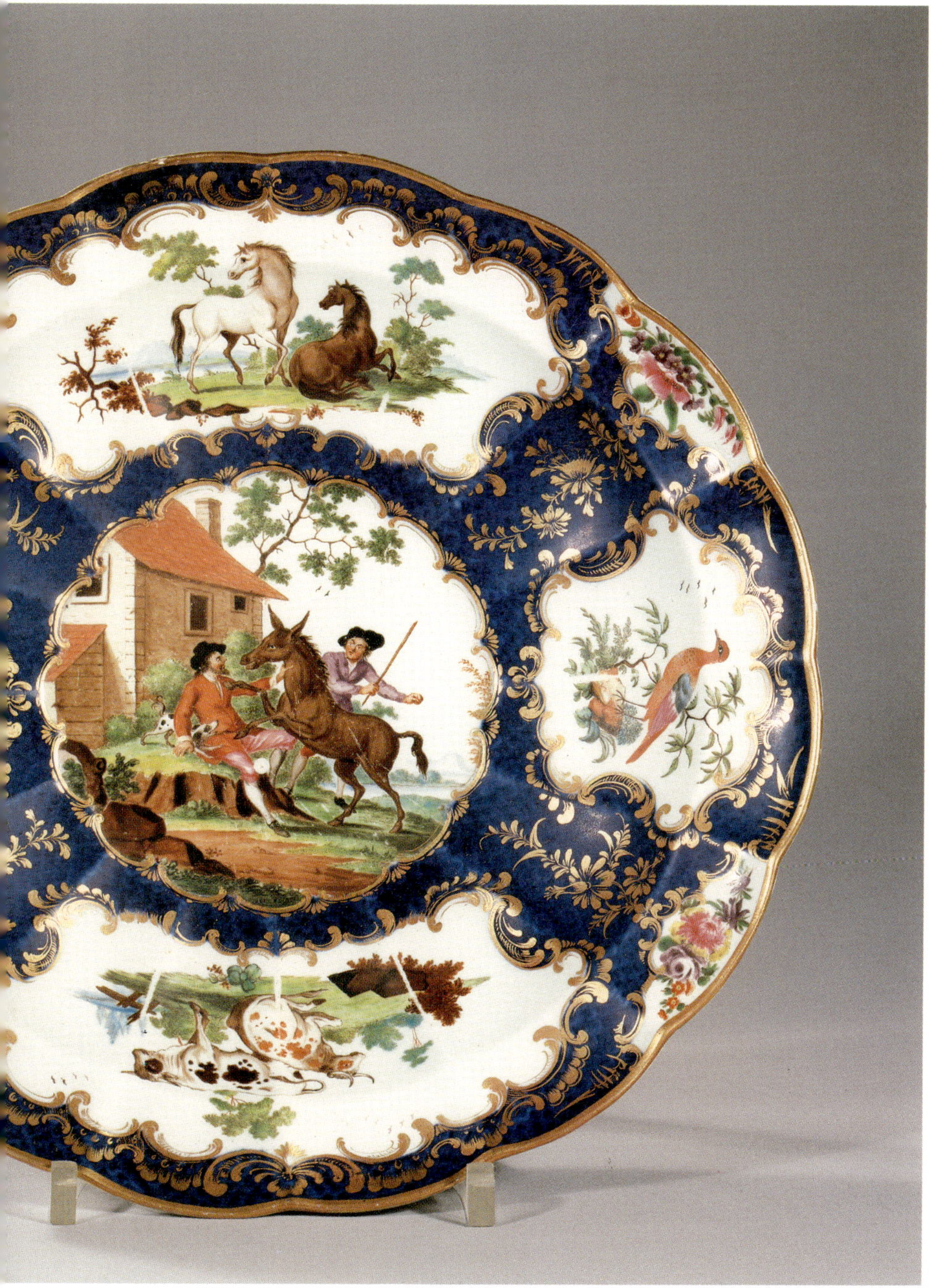

134 **Vase and cover** 1768–70
of ovoid shape, the white neck decorated with floral wreaths, on either side of the body are large oval panels, enclosed by a deep 'mazarine' blue ground with gilding. One reserve has a painting 'The Bather' based on one of that name by François le Moyne (1688–1737), painted 1724, now in the Hermitage, Leningrad. It was engraved (1731) by Laurent Cars, and reproduced in mezzotint by J. Johnson. The other large reserve has a bouquet of flowers, and there are also flowers in the two heart-shaped panels on the shoulders. The domed cover has two panels with birds.
At Waddesdon Manor there is a set of three green ground Sèvres vases (1765–70), on one of which the same scene is depicted. See the Waddesdon Catalogue – *Sèvres Porcelain* by S. Eriksen (1968), no. 73.
This vase was painted by John Donaldson (b. 1737, Edinburgh, d. 1801), who worked first in his home city where he painted fruit, flowers, landscapes and figures. In 1760 he moved to London, where he mainly painted portraits and miniatures, but also made etchings, and soon after his arrival began to decorate Chelsea porcelain. He is mentioned in Boswell's London Journal for Friday, 4 March 1763 – 'Donaldson, the painter drank tea with me. He reminded me of former days at Edinburgh . . . Donaldson is a kind of speculative being and must forsooth controvert established systems . . .' In 1764 and 1768 he obtained the premium given by the Society of Arts for the best picture in enamels. Barrett notes among the characteristics of Donaldson's painting 'a favourite rich puce, the stippling of the cheeks, well delineated features and lush foliage'.
Also in the collection is a garniture of three vases (nos. 115, 119 and 123) painted by Donaldson with equestrian scenes in the style of Philips Wouwerman of Haarlem (1619–68).

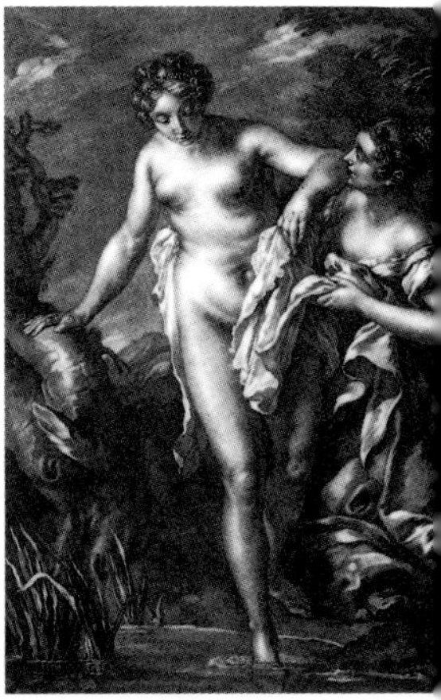

François le Moyne:
The Bather (mezzotint)

Height with cover 26.7 cm. Mark – fretted square.
Marshall, *op. cit.*, Plate 39, no. 825.

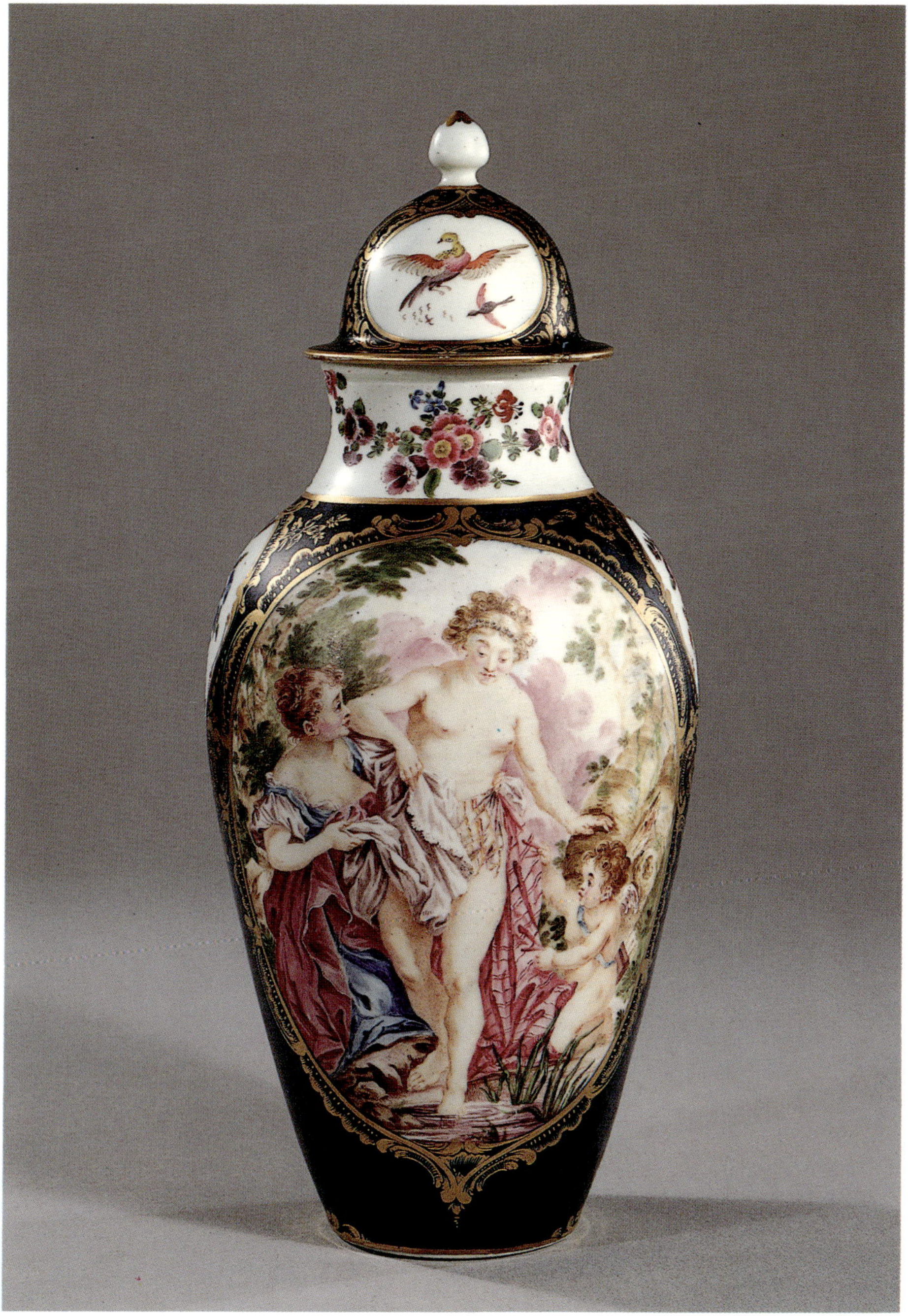

706 **Spoon tray** 1765–70
of hexagonal shape and fluted with a wavy gilt rim. The irregular apple-green border is defined by simple gilding. The central reserve is decorated in colours with spotted fruit and insects.
Apple-green is the most frequently found over-glaze ground colour. Notice the thickness of the enamel and the way the gilding lies beside and not on the green of this piece and the tureen on Plate 25a.

Length 15.2 cm. No mark.
Marshall, *op. cit.*, Plate 26, no. 589.

704 **Spoon tray** circa 1770
of hexagonal shape and fluted with wavy rim and gilt dentil edge. In the centre of the richly gilded light ruby ground is a heart-shaped reserve painted with a bird on a fruit spray.
The red enamel ground is very uneven and was probably applied in the London atelier of James Giles. It is interesting to compare the Giles and factory decoration in the central reserves. As with green grounds, this colour was often added to genuine Worcester pieces in the 19th century, as is probably the case with the tureen and cover (no. 452) with its dull red ground and heavy gilding.
A spoon tray was an essential part of a tea and coffee service at this period, and most Worcester examples are of this shape. Among the twenty spoon trays in the collection, however, two are ovoid (nos. 699 and 856), and two of a fluted lozenge shape (nos. 455 and 705).

Length 15.2 cm. No mark.
Marshall, *op. cit.*, Plate 26, no. 591.

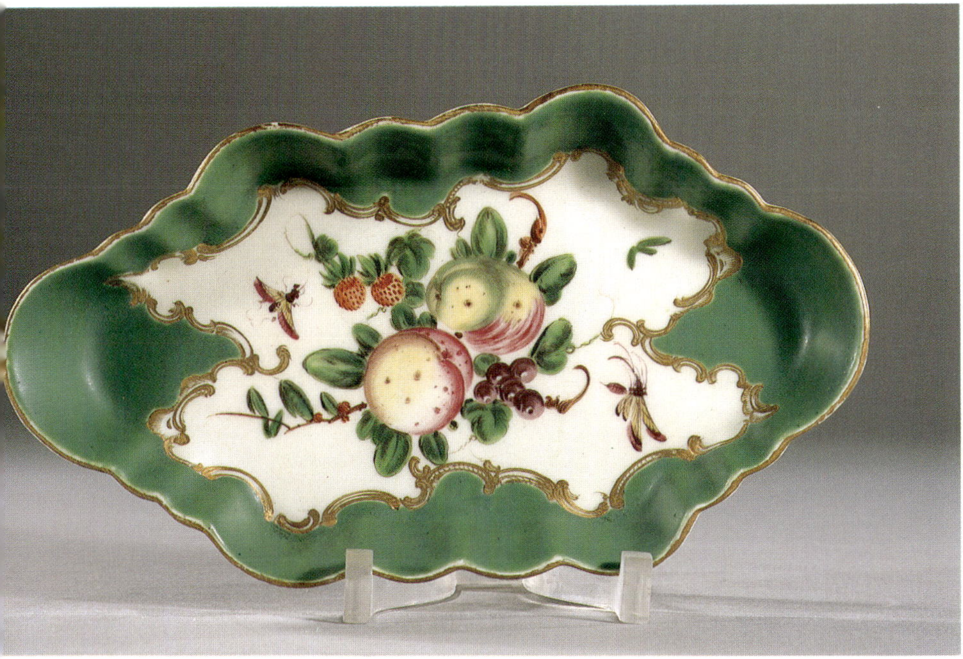

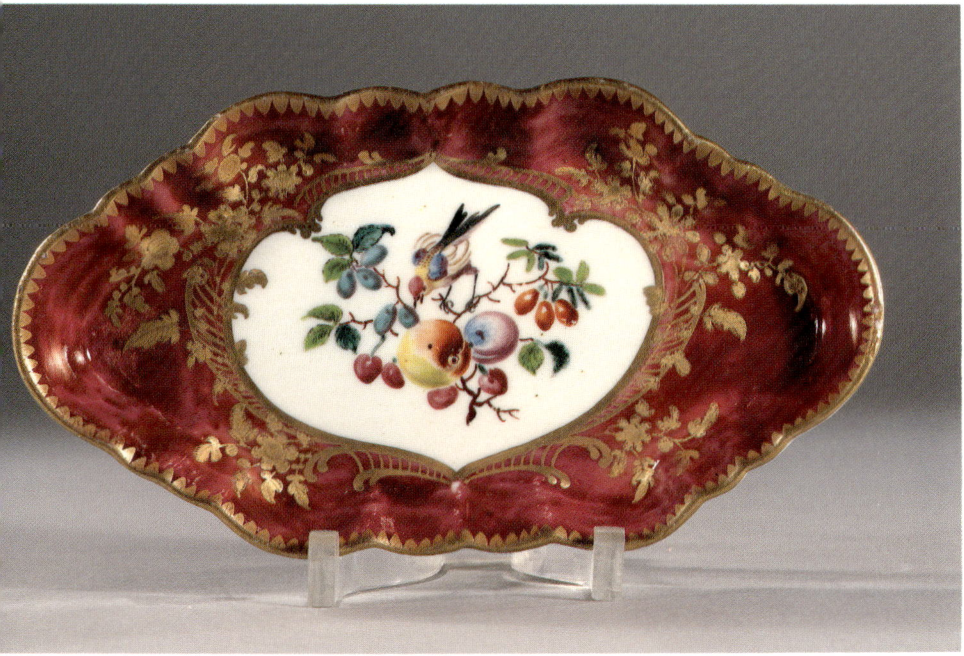

Plate 21

271 **Vase** 1765–70
of slender octagonal shape, with a wider band in the middle. Eight panels decorated with Japanese type flowers and birds, separated by orange and gilt patterned ribs. Round the base is an iron red border with white flowers in reserve. Gilt decoration above and below the central band. The interior has a border of scattered sprays of flowers.
This shape, called 'gu', was used for Chinese bronzes from the late Shang period, and copied by Chinese potters. The decoration is vaguely in the style of Japanese Kakiemon porcelain, though the large flowers are more reminiscent of Imari ware.
There are two similar vases in the Dyson Perrins Museum, together with a taller octagonal vase and cover. This one would also have formed part of a garniture. They are probably some of the biggest pieces attempted by the factory at this period, and evidently caused difficulties in firing, as can be seen by the slight deformation in shape.

Height 41 cm. No mark.
Marshall, *op. cit.*, Plate 41, no. 854.

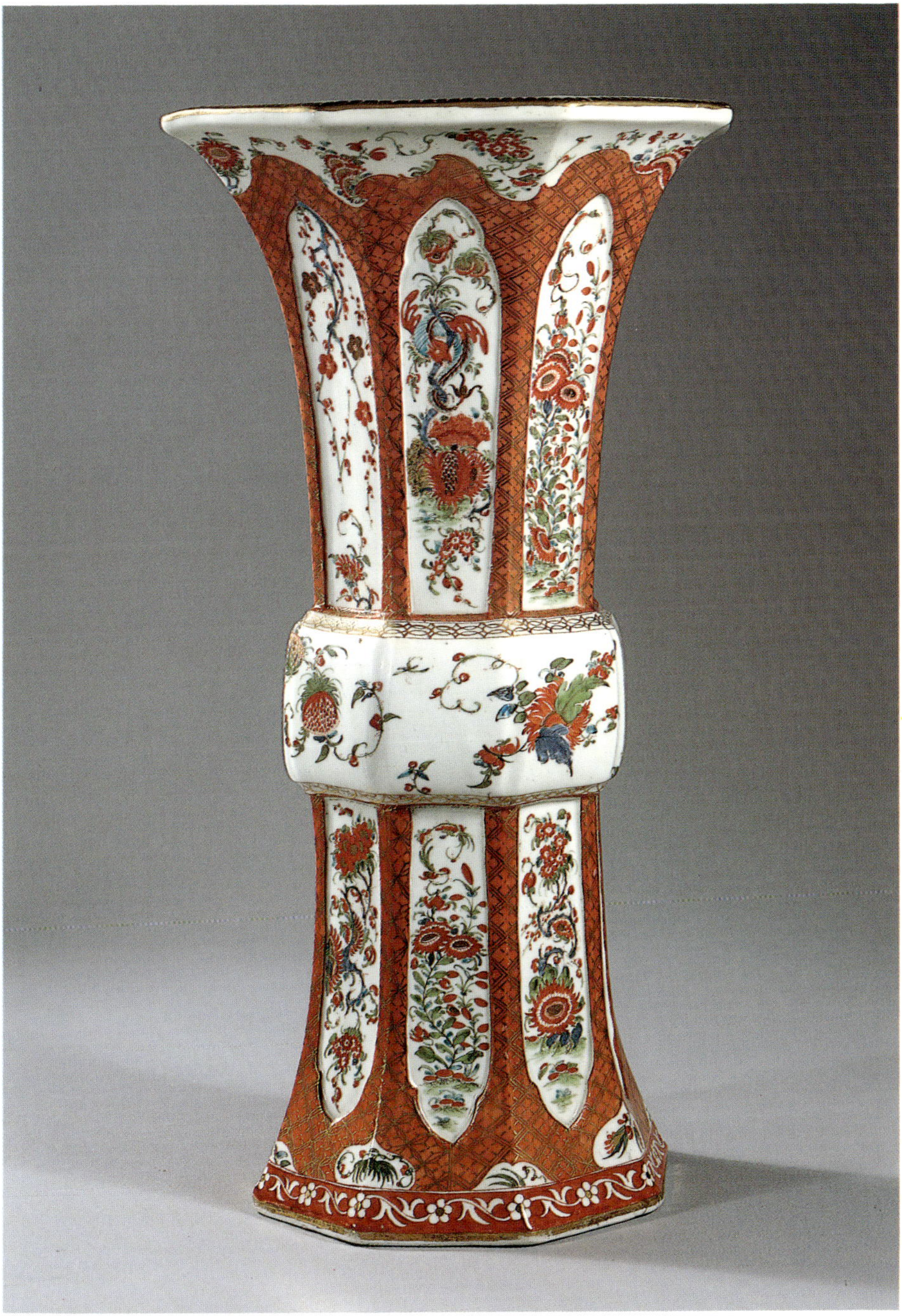

81 **Teapot and cover** 1770–75
of globular shape, with plain loop handle and domed cover with conical knop. Painted in colours with Mr Holland or Mr Smith as Iachimo in *Cymbeline* on one side, and Miss Pope as Doll Snip in *Harlequin's Invasion* on the other. Gilt border of ribbon with entwined leaves on cover, and gilt decoration on handle and spout.
For a full account of the Theatrical Service see *English Ceramic Circle Transactions*. Vol. 10, Part 5 (1980), pp. 272–292, 'The Worcester Theatrical Tea Service' by Babette Craven and Ian Lowe.
In Sayer and Bennett's catalogue of prints for 1775 were 'Dramatic Characters or 40 different portraits of Mr. Garrick and other capital Actors, . . . mostly from original drawings of De Fish and beautifully engraved by Charles Grignion, . . .' De Fish was Jean Louis Fesch (b. Basle, 1738) who was in England 1766–1773 and it was some of his drawings which were copied for this service. The Sayer print for Iachimo was labelled Mr Holland in 1771, but Mr (Gentleman) Smith in 1773. The former played Iachimo from 1761 to 1769 at Drury Lane, and the latter from 1767 to 1774 at Covent Garden, then transferred to Drury Lane. Miss Jane Pope was in *Harlequin's Invasion* by David Garrick from 1769 to 1796. When the above article was written nine pieces of this service were known including a saucer dish in the Manchester City Art Gallery, showing Mr Reddish as Posthumus in *Cymbeline* (Leary and Walton, *op. cit.*, no. 84), and a bowl in the Dyson Perrins Museum with Mr Dunstall as Hodge in *Love in a Village*, and Mrs Bellamy as Clarinda in *The Suspicious Husband* (see opposite).

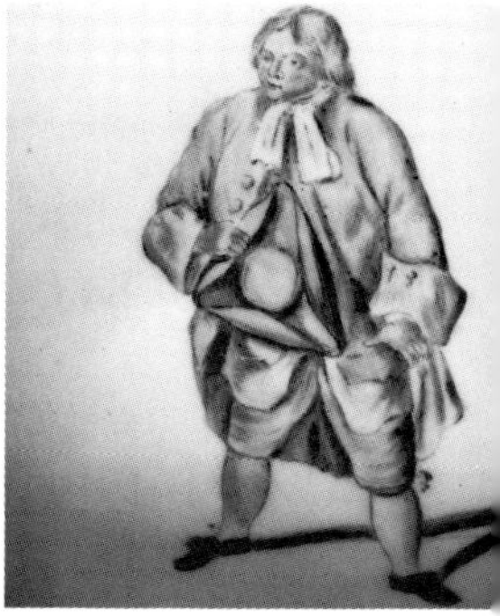

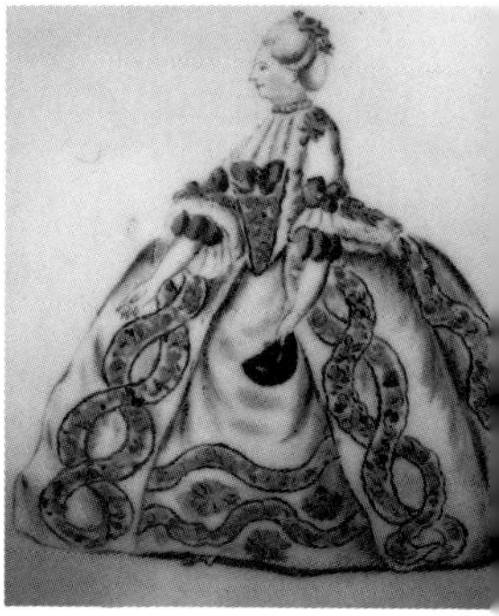

Height with cover 15 cm. No mark.
Marshall, *op. cit.*, Colour Plate 28, Plate 19, no. 349.
Barrett, *op. cit.*, Plate 68b.

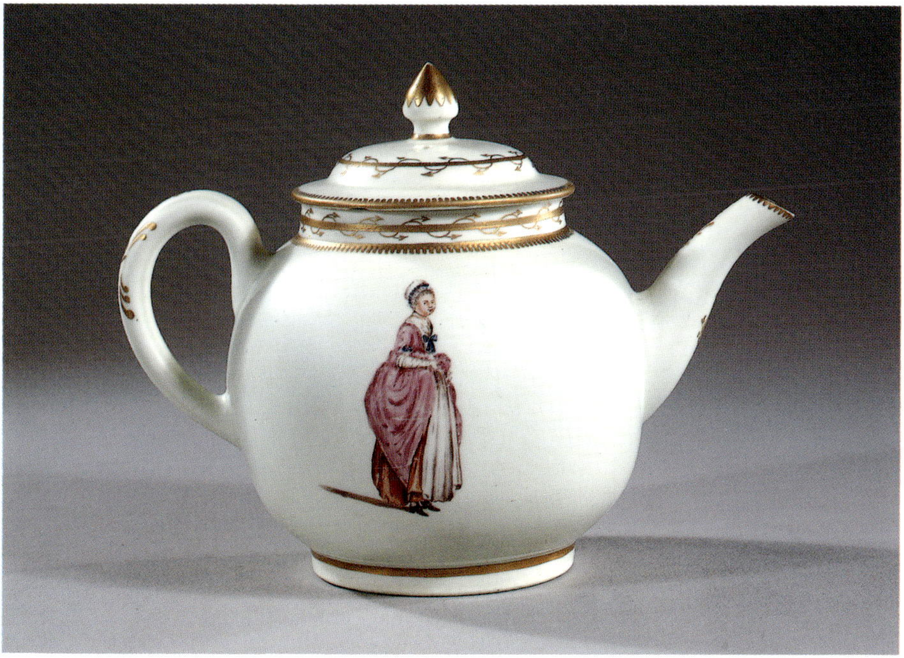

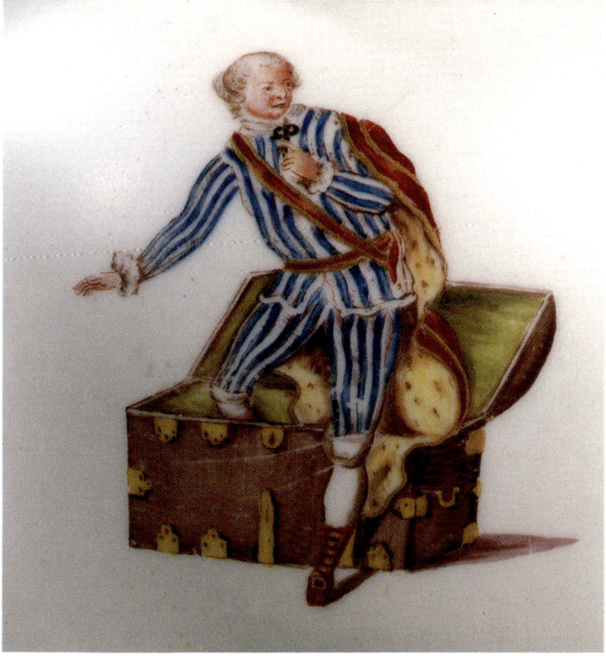

83 **Teapot and cover** 1772
of globular shape, with a gilded, plain loop handle and spout, and a gilt dentil border round the base of the neck. Painted in soft colours with two lovers seated beside an urn on a pedestal which is signed 'F Duvivier/in(venit) ins(cripsit)/1772' and on the other with two more lovers and a sheep in front of ruins, and also signed 'Duvill???ier/1772'. Domed cover with gilt decoration and open rosebud finial.
The style of Fidèle Duvivier, who was born in Tournai in 1740, suggests that he worked in the factory there before coming to London about 1763 or 1764, where he either worked at Chelsea (replacing a cousin who went to Tournai) or for James Giles. He was under contract to William Duesbury of Derby from 31 October 1769, 'To work as a porcelain painter and roses (*sic*) for 4 years at 24/- per week and an extra 5 guineas if Mr. Duesbury considered he merited it'. He continued to work in London but was in Derby before March, 1771. As the gilding is in the style of Giles's atelier, Duvivier probably decorated this teapot there. His work is also found on New Hall (signed piece), Caughley, Turner of Lane End (signed piece) and Sceaux. See *English Ceramic Circle Transactions*, Vol. 11, Part 1 (1981), pp. 12–20, 'Fidelle (*sic*) Duvivier paints New Hall', by David Holgate.

Height with cover 14.4 cm. No mark.
Marshall, *op. cit.*, Colour Plate 29, Plate 19, no. 345.
Barrett, *op. cit.*, Plate 69b and page 55.
Milk jug with similar decoration Albert Amor, 1976, *op. cit.*, no. 70, and illustrated Barrett, *op. cit.*, Plate 69a.

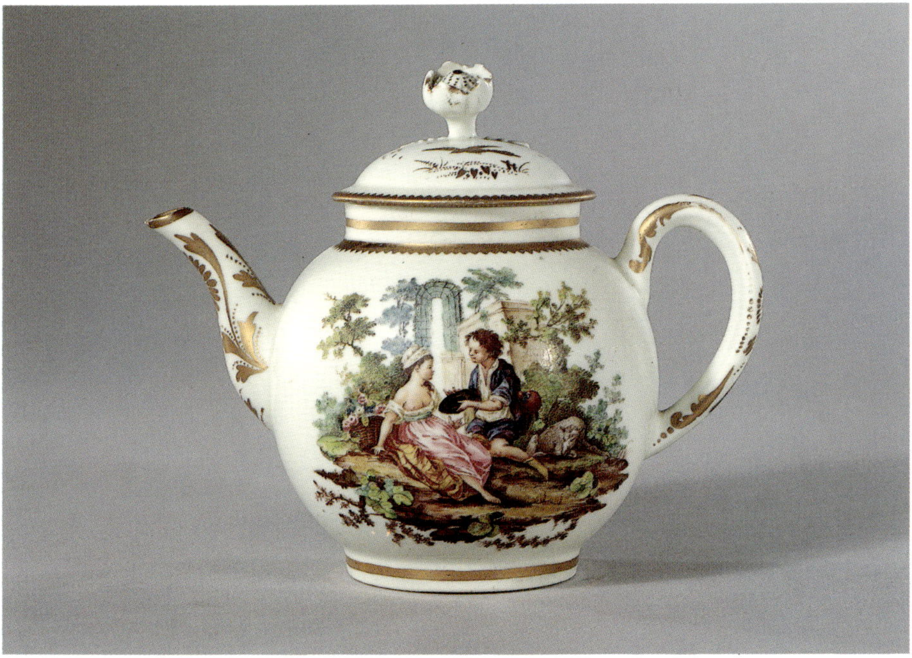

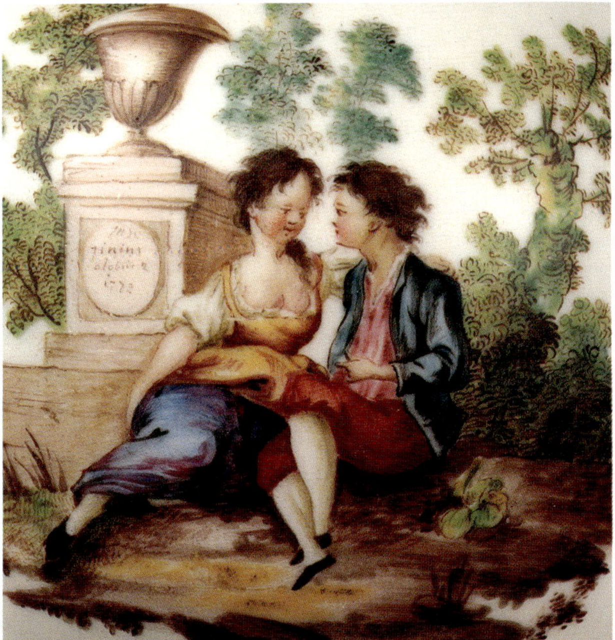

Plate 24

239 **Potpourri vase and cover** circa 1775
of goblet shape, with pierced lattice work band under the rim, below which are straight sides defined by a gilt moulding, above rounded sides of the baluster style, and then a spreading foot. The cover, which has a gilt dentil border, also has a pierced lattice work band and is surmounted by a knop in the form of a gilt bunch of grapes with leaves. The entire decoration is of 'dry' blue bouquets and sprays of flowers, which, though brighter in colour, are inspired by Vincennes porcelain.

Height with cover 28cm. No mark.
Marshall, *op. cit.*, Plate 15, no. 262.
Sandon, *op. cit.*, Plate 120 shows a differently shaped potpourri vase which has a similar grape knop and 'dry' blue floral decoration.

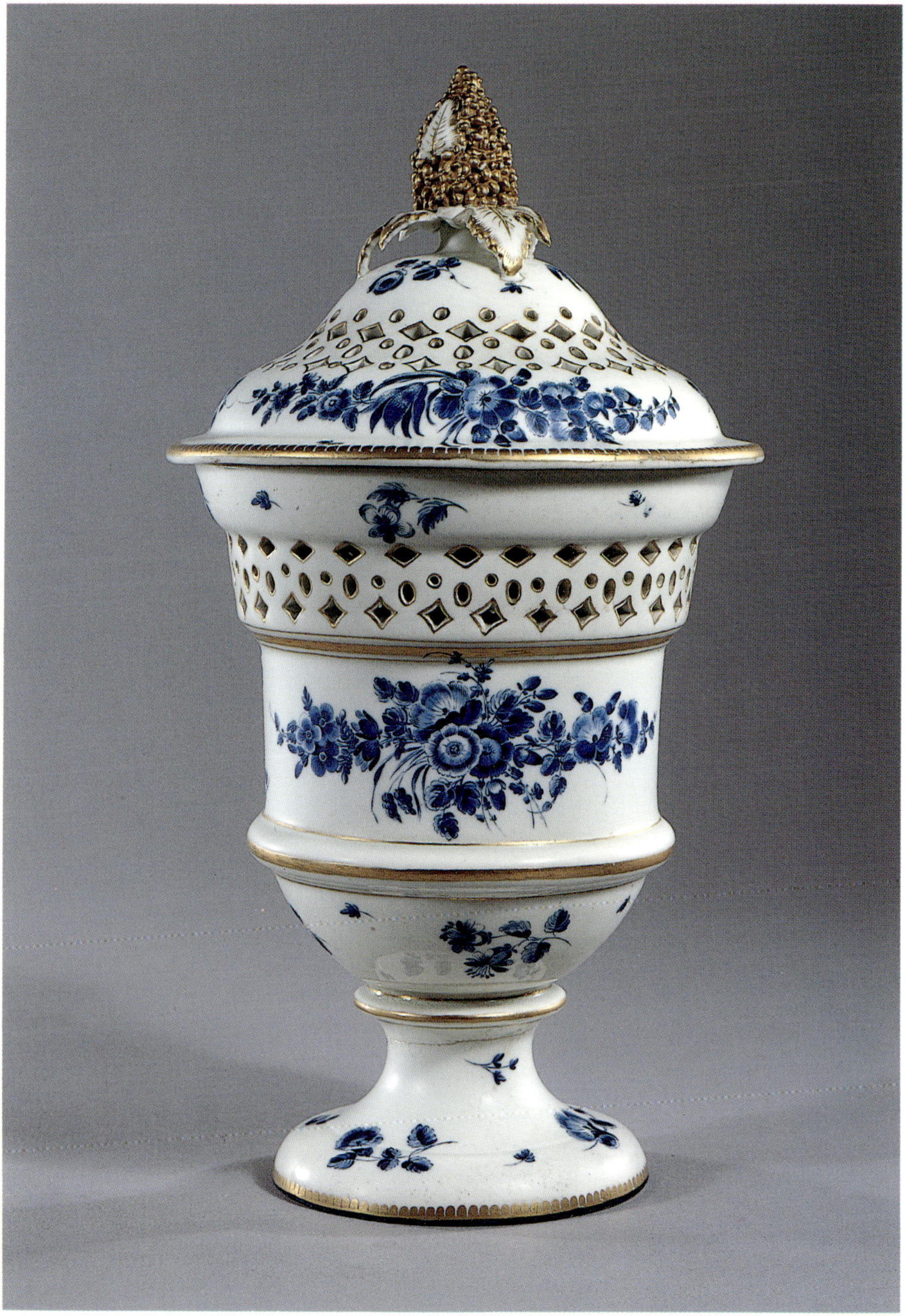

Plate 25

433 **Tureen, cover, stand and ladle** 1768–72
of oval shape. The tureen has two moulded shell handles, while the cover is surmounted by an artichoke knop with stalk and two leaves. The ladle has a rounded bowl and curved shank. Each piece has an irregular green border edged with gilt scrolls, from which depend two floral wreaths and flower sprays.
This is called the 'Marchioness of Huntley pattern', because a dessert service in it was sold by the second wife of the 10th Marquess in 1882.
No. 451, a small plate, has the same decoration.
Many green ground pieces are regarded with suspicion, for instance the mug (no. 436) which, though inscribed 'Mr. Beng^{n}. Giles May ye 16, 1772' is now thought to have been decorated later.

Length of stand 23.5 cm, height of tureen and cover 12.7 cm. No marks.
Marshall, *op. cit.*, Plate 34, no. 737.
Spero, *op. cit.*, no. 101 is a plate with the same pattern.

902 **Tureen, cover and stand** 1775–80
of the same shape as no. 433 above. Richly decorated in colours with finely painted fruit, flowers and insects. 'Duke of Gloucester service'.
This is one of the finest services produced during the First Period at the factory. It is said to have been made for William Henry, Duke of Gloucester (1743–1805), third son of Frederick, Prince of Wales. Seventy pieces were included in the Duke of Cambridge sale at Christie's in 1904. The painted decoration, which is in the style of gold anchor Chelsea, has sometimes been attributed to James Giles, but this now seems unlikely.

Length of stand 23.5 cm, height of tureen and cover 11.5 cm. Mark – solid gold crescent on tureen and stand.
Other pieces from this service are illustrated as follows: Barrett, *op. cit.*, Plate 54 plate; Sandon, *op. cit.*, Colour Plate IV, large tureen; Spero, *op. cit.*, no. 64 tureen stand; Albert Amor, 1984, *The Wills Collection*, No. 77 plate, 1985, *op. cit.*, no. 73 plate.

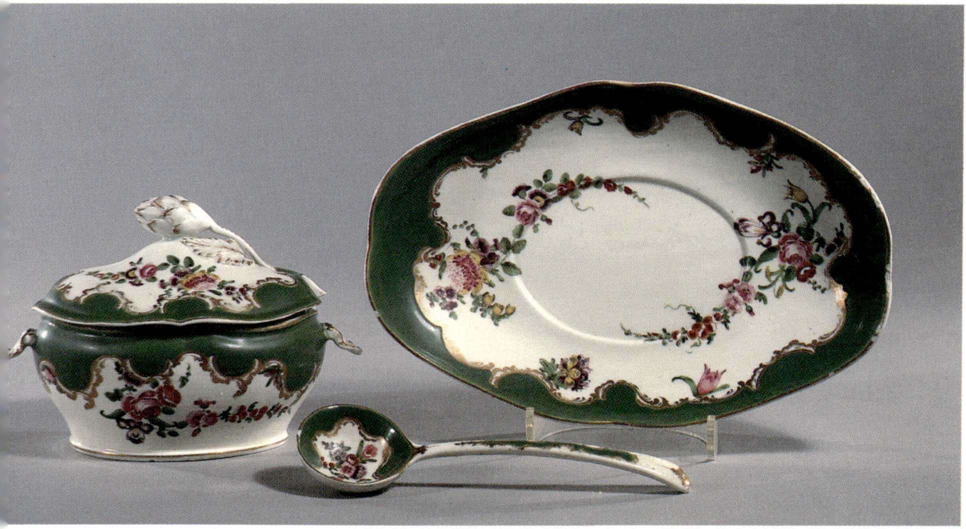

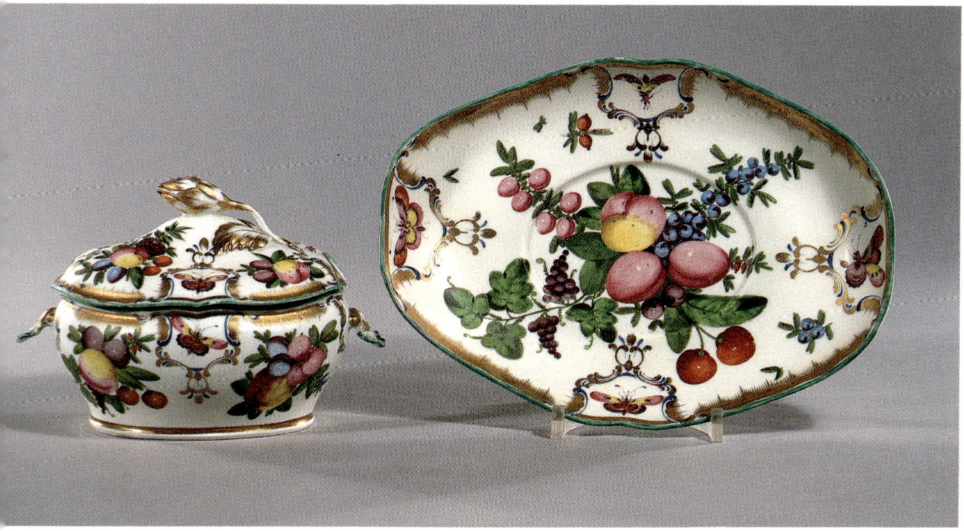

28 **Plate** circa 1775
with a fluted border and narrow royal blue band edged with gilt scrolls. The centre decorated in colours with exotic birds in a landscape, surrounded by flying birds and insects.
A service in this pattern was owned by Admiral Lord Rodney (1719–92), which is why his name is linked with it. This style of bird painting in a landscape was done at Sèvres.

Diameter 21.6 cm. Mark – open underglaze blue crescent.
Marshall, *op. cit.*, Plate 16, no. 277.
A plate from the same service is illustrated in Spero, *op. cit.*, no. 142.

30 **Plate** circa 1775
with a fluted border and royal blue band gilded with cable and trellis patterns. Decorated in the centre in colours with a river landscape surrounded by a gilt and turquoise husk circle, around which are clusters of fruit and flying birds.
A dish with similar decoration is illustrated in Spero, *op. cit.*, no. 140. This pattern is associated with Lord Henry Thynne, who may have been either the second son (1797–1837) of the 2nd Marquess of Bath, and later 3rd Marquess, or the latter's second son (1832–1904), but the reason is unknown.
These late patterns with their royal blue borders show clearly the strong Sèvres influence on the Worcester decoration in the 1770's.

Diameter 21.7 cm. Mark – solid underglaze blue crescent.
Marshall, *op. cit.*, Plate 25, no. 472.

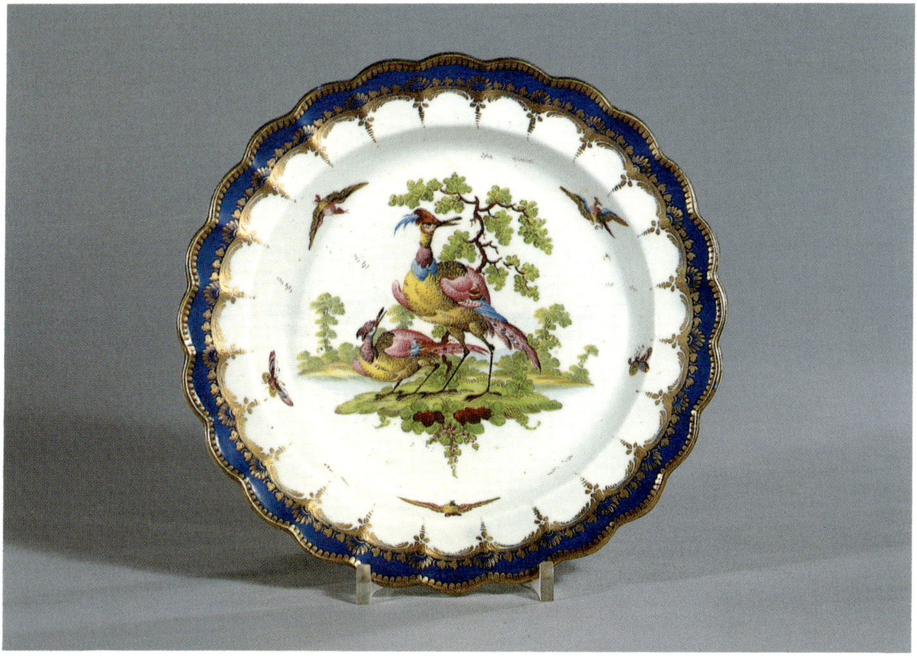

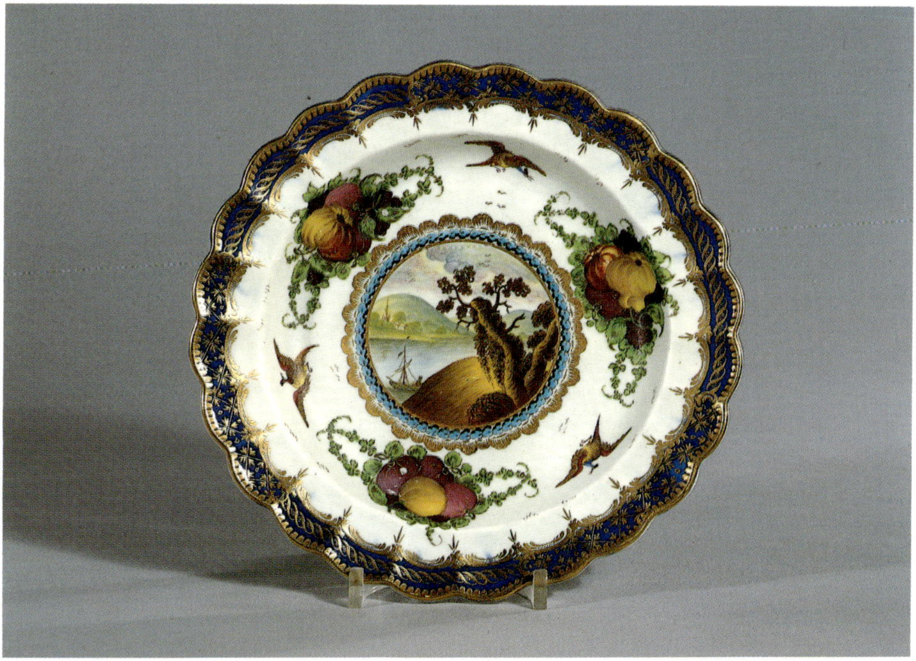

Plate 27

369 **Chocolate cup and saucer** circa 1775

The reeded cup and fluted saucer have gilt rims, and the cup two entwined twig handles. Each is painted with four groups of pink and gilt trellis-work linked by festoons of berried hops, above and below which is a gilt-edged turquoise scale border.

This is one of the many Sèvres inspired 'Hop Trellis patterns', which also occur with borders in pink no. 72, royal blue no. 8, green no. 448, while no. 194 is a Sèvres example with next to it the Worcester copy, no. 195. The entwined handle also derives from Sèvres and was used at Worcester from the late 1760's.

Diameter of cup 7 cm, of saucer 14 cm. No marks.
Marshall, *op. cit.*, Plate 28, no. 622.
Spero, *op. cit.*, illustrates a bowl with the same decoration, no. 106.

931 **Dish** circa 1775

of lozenge shape with a wavy gilt dentil edge and fluted border with alternating panels of purple shagreen, floral gilding, pink herringbone, and turquoise lattice-work. In the centre is a landscape with two exotic birds, in the manner of Sèvres.

This tea and coffee service, which also shows clearly the influence of Sèvres, once belonged to the celebrated Edwardian hostess, Mrs Arthur James.

Length 29.5 cm. No mark.
Marshall, *op. cit.*, Plate 31, no. 690.
Tea cup, coffee cup and saucer from this service exhibited Albert Amor, 1984, *op. cit.*, no. 89. Spero, *op. cit.*, illustrates an oval dish no. 103, and tea cup and saucer no. 107.

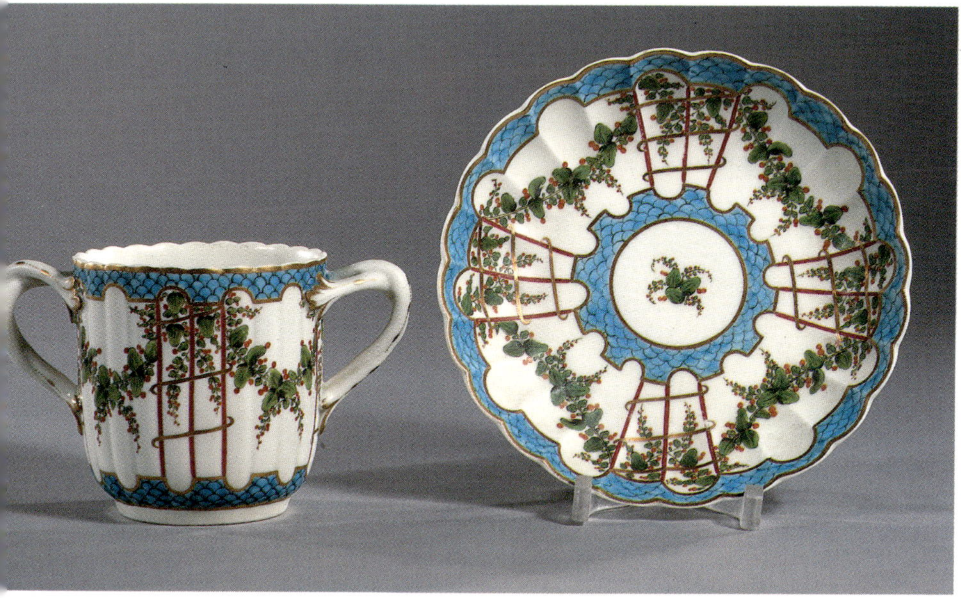

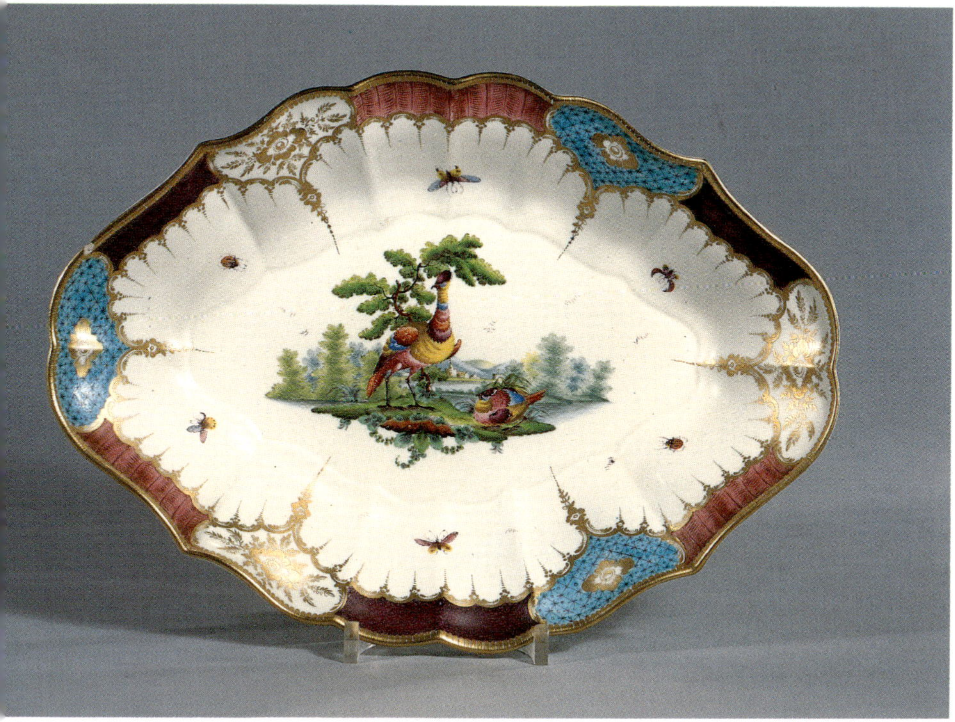

505 and 506 **Vases** 1762–65
from a garniture of five. One is ovoid shaped with a cover, and the other of bronze beaker shape. Painted in colours with semi-naturalistic birds perched in leafy branches and with scattered sprays of European flowers.
It is unusual to find a complete garniture of this type which has some of the most important examples of the naturalistic bird painting from the James Giles atelier. See Anne George's article 'A Question of Attribution' in *The Antique Dealer and Collector's Guide*, May 1987, pp. 44–48.
James Giles, who was of Huguenot stock, was the son of a 'China Painter', and was apprenticed to a jeweller in 1733. Between 1745 and 1756 he appears to have worked in Worcester, before returning to London, where in 1767 he made an arrangement with the Worcester factory to be supplied with white porcelain to decorate. This arrangement ended in 1771, after which Giles experienced financial difficulties, due also to the death of his partner. William Duesbury of Derby bought extensively at the sale in 1776 of Giles's goods, and took over the balance of his stock and fixed assets.
In March 1774 a five day sale was held at Christie's of the 'Stock in Trade of Mr. James Giles, Chinaman and Enameller . . . consisting of Many superb and select Articles of the India, Chelsea, Derby, Worcester and Frankendahl Porcelain . . .'

Height of vase with cover 22 cm, of beaker 15.2 cm. No marks.
Marshall, *op. cit.*, Plate 32, no. 698.
No. 505 exhibited Albert Amor, 1983, *The Elegant Porcelain of James Giles*, no. 74.

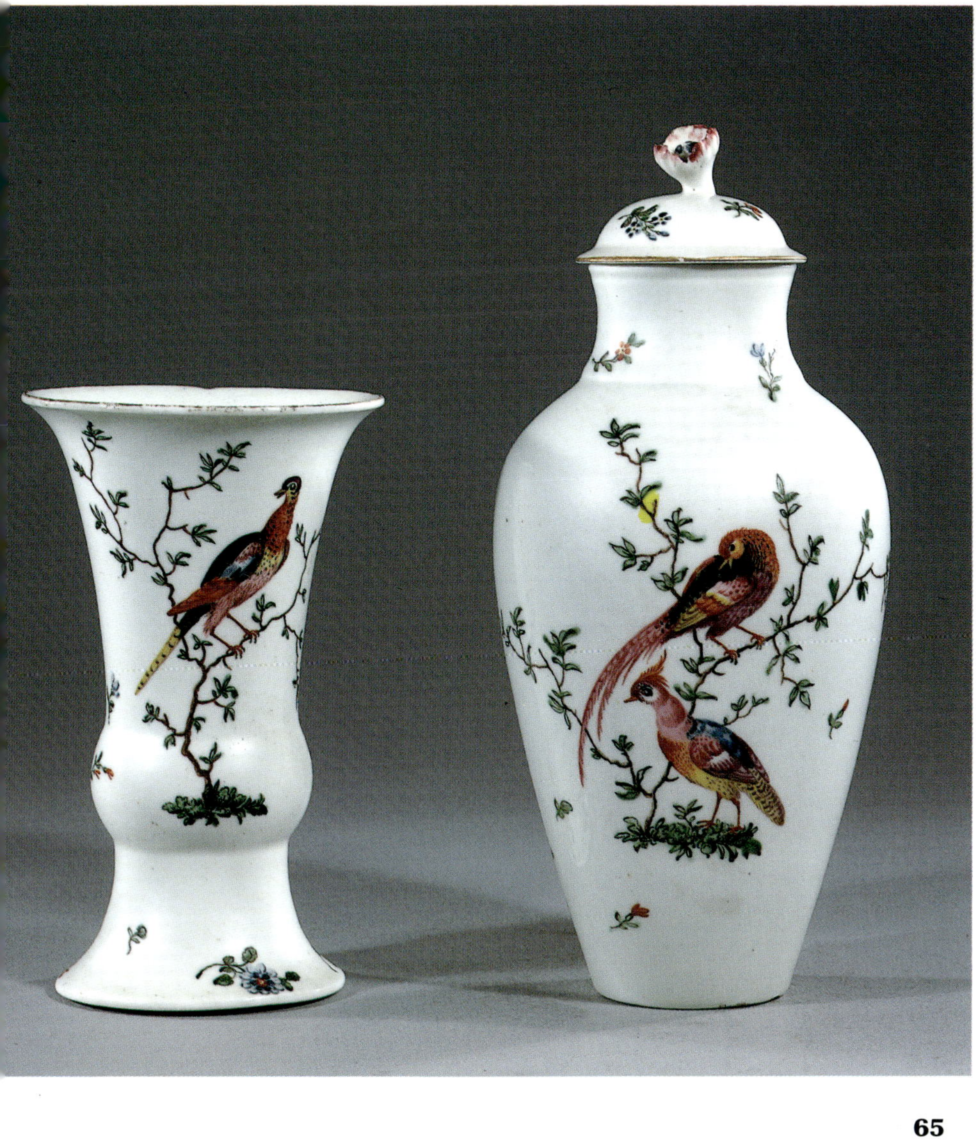

Plate 29

127 **Tea caddy** circa 1770
of ovoid shape. The blue scale ground decorated with ciselé gilt flowers. Two large reserves painted in colours, with, on one side a girl blowing bubbles, and on the other fruit and flowers. Smaller reserves have flowers. The cover is missing.

One of a pair of tea caddies known to have belonged to James Giles's daughter, Mary, who married John Hall, line engraver. Their daughter married John Eustace Grubbe, whose descendant Miss M. J. M. Grubbe sold the caddies at Sotheby's on 13 May 1952. They are usually accepted as having been painted in Giles's atelier. It is from the painting on these, and on the Grubbe plates in the Victoria and Albert Museum, that many other pieces have been attributed to the atelier. Miss Grubbe presented Giles's ledger, covering the years 1771 to 1776, to the English Ceramic Circle in 1952. Mr Marshall calculated that the Giles atelier decorated more than 40,000 pieces of Worcester porcelain during the years 1771 to 1774. This would mean that between 1767 and 1775 the output from the atelier of polychrome Worcester exceeded that of the factory.

The high standard of the gilding on many pieces attributed to Giles may have derived from his apprenticeship to a jeweller.

Height 12 cm. Mark – fretted square.
Marshall, *op. cit.*, Colour Plate 10, Plate 43, no. 901.
Barrett, *op. cit.*, Plate 68a; G. Coke, *In Search of James Giles*, Plate 41a.
The companion tea caddy, which shows a boy reaching for a bird, exhibited Albert Amor, 1977, *James Giles*, no. 5, and 1983, *op. cit.*, no. 9.

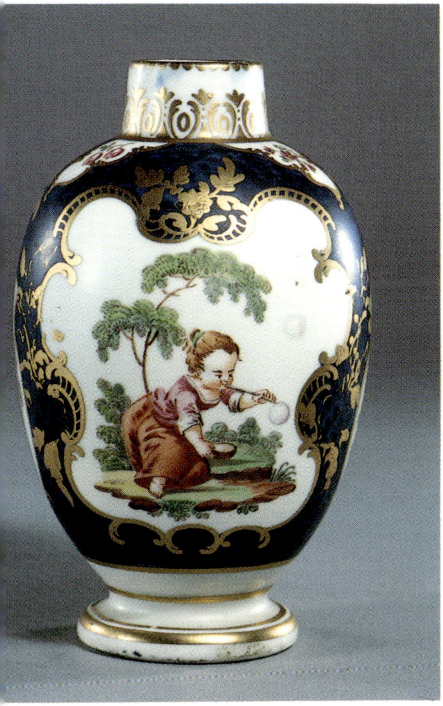

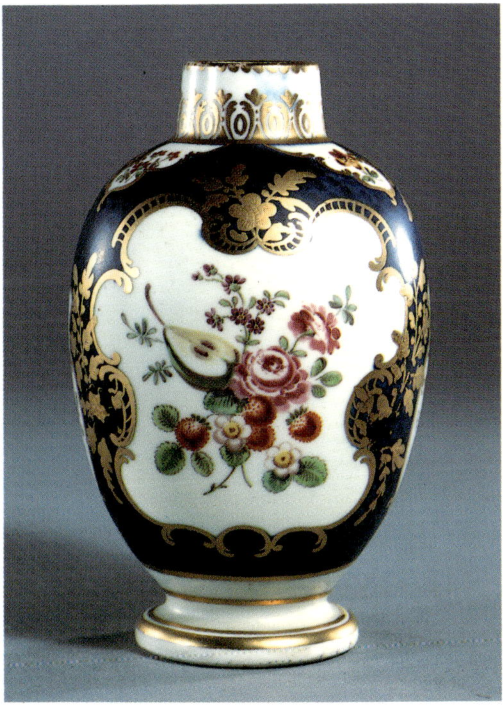

Plate 30

52 **Plate** circa 1770
painted in carmine monochrome, the centre with a European landscape of classical ruins and a farmhouse with tower, and sheep. The border is edged with gilt and decorated with sprays of flowers, including a divergent tulip.
The cup and saucer, no. 65, has the same style of carmine landscape, which is also on one of the four plates (see below) presented to the Victoria and Albert Museum by Mrs D. E. Grubbe in 1935.

Diameter 22.4 cm. No mark.
Marshall, *op. cit.*, Part I, Plate 7c.
The companion plate, illustrated in Spero, *op. cit.*, no. 147, was sold by Mr Marshall in 1953.
Similar exhibited Albert Amor, 1980, *The Golden Age*, no. 63 and 1983, *op. cit.*, no. 5.

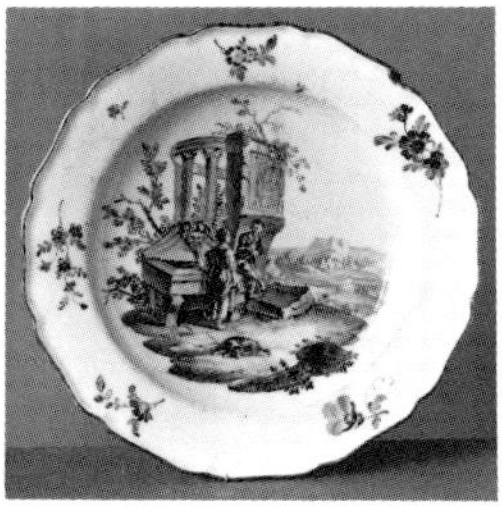

51 **Basket** circa 1775
of oval shape, the sides formed by interlacing strapwork, with applied pink and blue rosettes on the outside. Gilt branch handles at the base of which are applied flowers. Centre painted in colours with a cluster of fruit and flowers and round the top an irregular pink scale border. This pink scale ground was used by Giles, in imitation of Meissen (see no. 192) on Worcester, Caughley and Neale porcelain (no. 193).

Length 26 cm. No mark.
Marshall, *op. cit.*, Part I, Plate 8e, and Part II, Plate 42, no. 856. Similar exhibited Albert Amor, 1983, *op. cit.*, no. 44, and illustrated Coke, *op. cit.*, frontispiece.

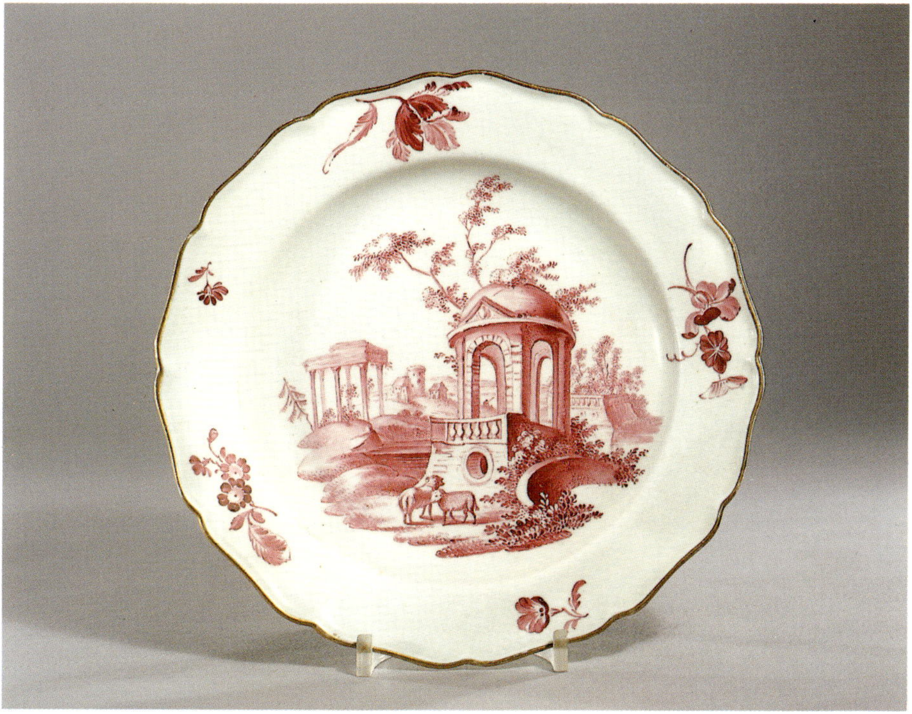

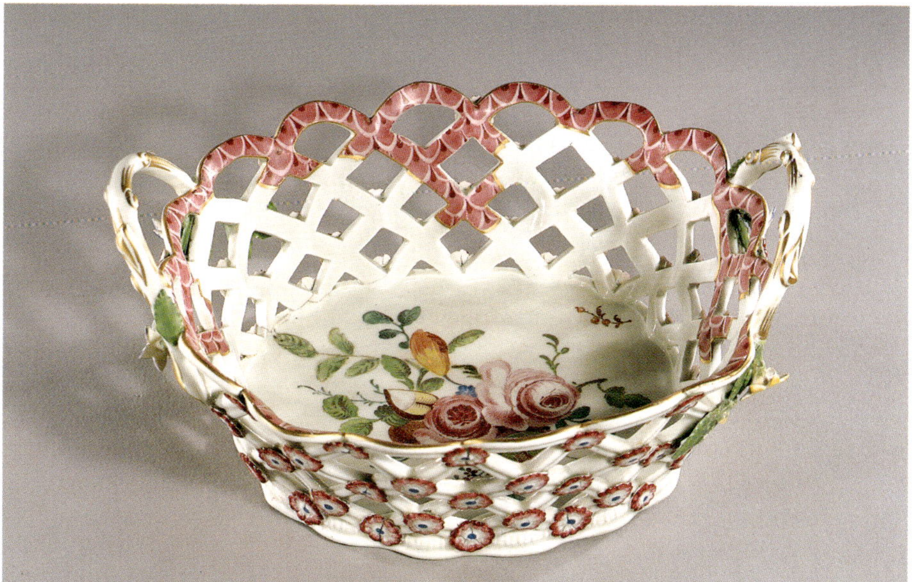

Plate 31

126 **Sucrier and cover** circa 1767–68
with a powder blue ground on which are three fan shaped reserves painted in colours with European musicians and smaller circular reserves with insects. The ground decorated with flower sprays in ciselé gilding. Rosebud finial on the domed cover. Spray of berries inside the bowl.
As a service in this pattern was owned by an Earl of Dudley, it is called the 'Lord Dudley pattern'.
Powder blue was probably the first underglaze blue ground to be introduced and was used with overglaze colours by the middle 1760's. The typical fan shaped reserves were inspired by Chinese designs.
The musicians are nearer to the Watteau style than to Teniers, which is represented by the tea caddy (Plate 29), both having been painted in the Giles atelier.

Height 10.5 cm. No mark.
Marshall, *op. cit.*, Plate 19, no. 352.
Other pieces in this pattern illustrated Barrett, *op. cit.*, Plate 74a, Coke, *op. cit.*, 45a, Spero, *op. cit.*, no. 157, Albert Amor, 1977, *op. cit.*, no. 50, 1983, *op. cit.*, no. 37.

577 **Dessert dish** circa 1770–72
of fluted square shape, the blue scale ground profusely gilt with flowers and foliage in ciselé gilding. The four rococo reserves painted in colours with exotic birds, while the smaller claw shaped reserves have flowers. In the centre a circular panel of flowers.
It is not known why this pattern is named after Lady Mary Wortley Montagu, who had died in 1762, before it was introduced.

Diameter 22.4 cm. Mark – fretted square.
Marshall, *op. cit.*, Part I, Plate 9d, Part II, Plate 38, no. 811.
Similar exhibited Albert Amor, 1984, *op. cit.*, no. 70, and the cup and saucer (no. 557) in the same pattern, exhibited Albert Amor, 1983, *op. cit.*, no. 40.
For other variants of this pattern see Coke, *op. cit.*, p. 164, Colour Plate II, and Plates 38 and 39.

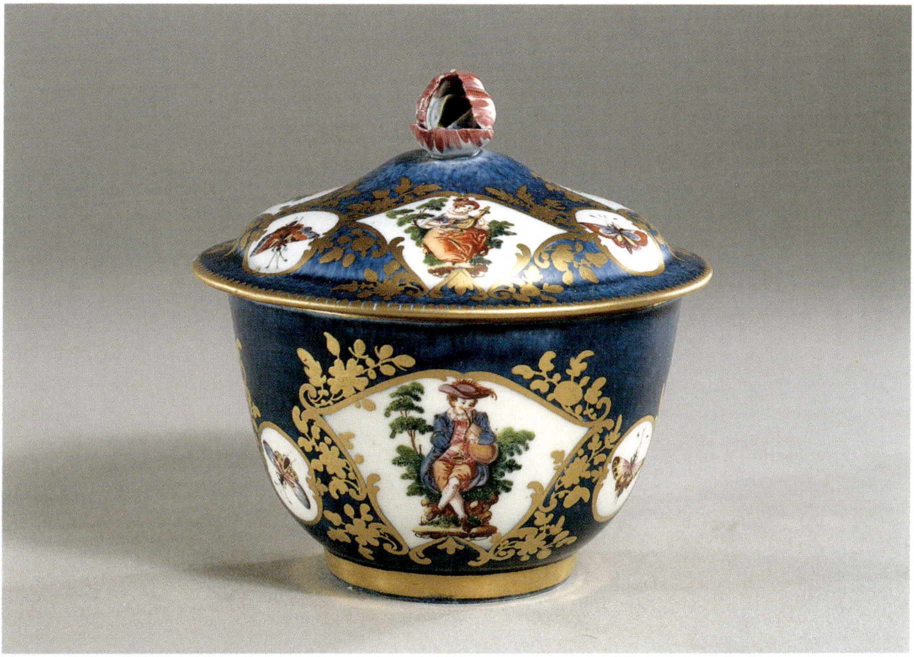

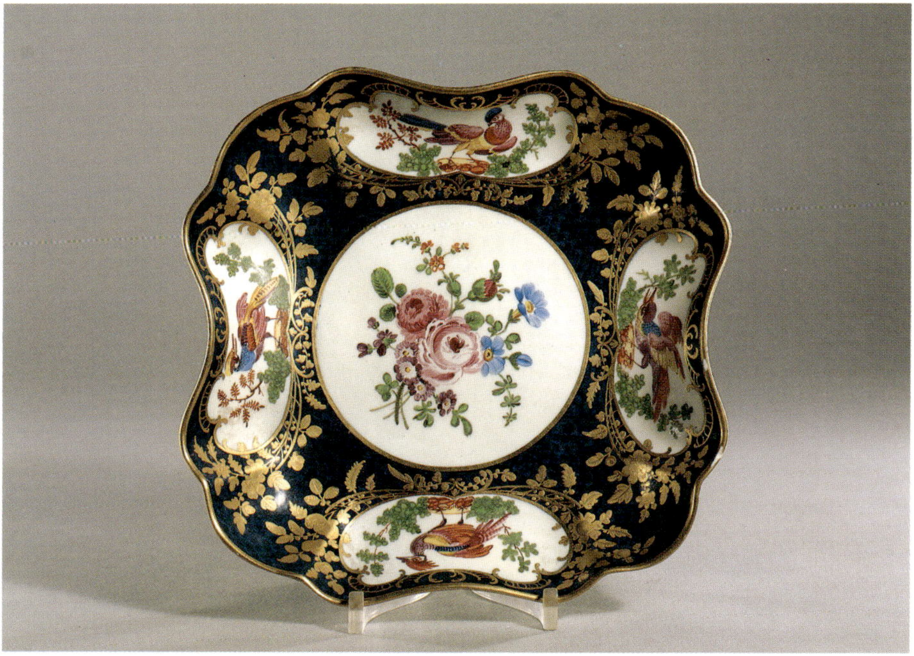

Plate 32

414 **Chocolate cup and saucer** circa 1770–72
of ogee shape, with two pierced gilt handles. Large bouquets and sprays of flowers in the style of Meissen inside and outside cup and on saucer.
An example of the finest Meissen style flower painting from the Giles atelier. The divergent tulip, so often depicted by Giles and which is frequently seen on Mennecy porcelain, also appears on the carmine plate Plate 30. The ogee shape cup was made from the middle 1760's.

Diameter of cup 9.8 cm, of saucer 14.8 cm. No mark.
Marshall, *op. cit.*, Colour Plate 8, Plate 16, no. 286.
Exhibited Albert Amor, 1977, *op. cit.*, no. 73.
Barrett, *op. cit.*, Plate 66. Spero, *op. cit.*, illustrates companion cup and saucer, no. 159, sold by Mr Marshall in 1953.

401 **Porringer, cover and stand** 1770–72
of reeded design with two moulded scroll handles. The lightly domed cover is surmounted by a pink flower finial. Painted in colours with a wreath of flowers entwined about a gilt line.
It is unusual to find a porringer with both cover and stand. This one is an example of Giles's decoration in the manner of Sèvres, and forms a contrast with no. 414.

Diameter of stand 15.6 cm, height of porringer and cover 12.7 cm. No mark.
Marshall, *op. cit.*, Colour Plate 30, Plate 16, no. 288.
Similar stand exhibited Albert Amor, 1983, *op. cit.*, no. 16, and illustrated Coke, *op. cit.*, Plate 2b.

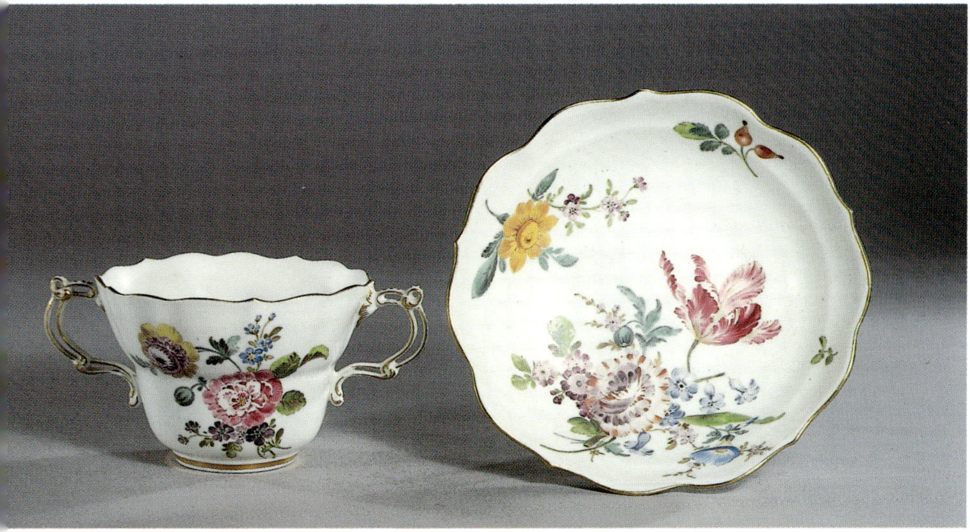

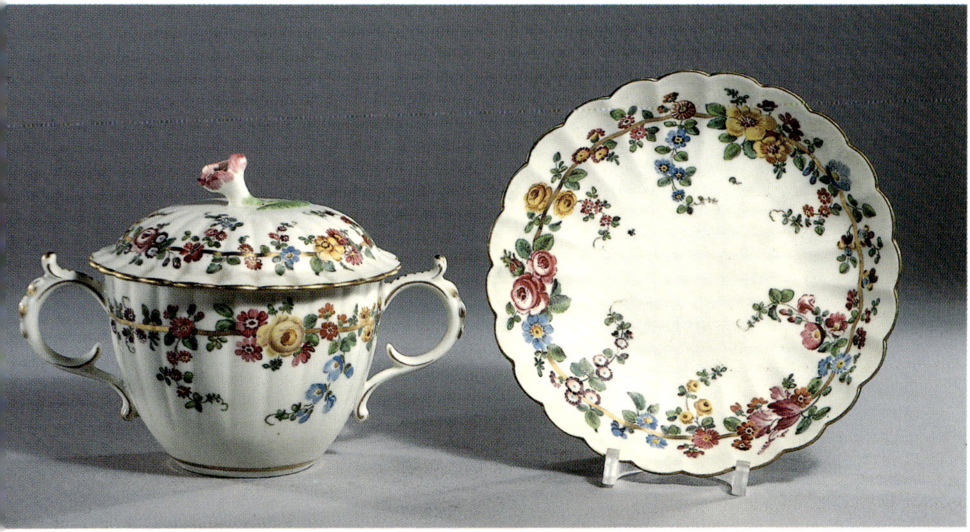

Plate 33

366 **Plate** circa 1770
with scalloped edge, the solid turquoise ground is decorated with three gilt scroll bordered reserves, each containing a different design – exotic bird and fruit; bouquets of flowers between double blue lines; and swags of green monochrome flowers. In the centre a gilt and white whorl, part of the 'Queen's pattern'.
This plate and the similar one at the British Museum (see below) were thought to be Giles 'pattern' plates until the discovery by Christie's of a bowl (see Coke, *op. cit.*, p. 165 and Plate 41c, exhibited Albert Amor, 1983, *op. cit.*, no. 1) decorated in the same manner. On the three pieces there are a total of six different patterns.
In this collection the 'Queen's pattern' appears on no. 945, and the flowers with blue lines on no. 1052, which also has auriculas, as on this plate, and on so many other pieces painted in Giles's atelier.

Diameter 21 cm. Mark – gold anchor.
Marshall, *op. cit.*, Part I, Plate 10a, Part II, Plate 28, no. 626.
Exhibited Albert Amor, 1977, *op. cit.*, no. 54.

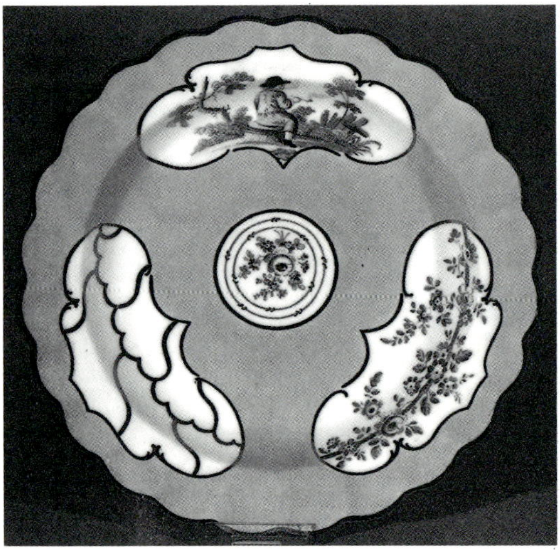

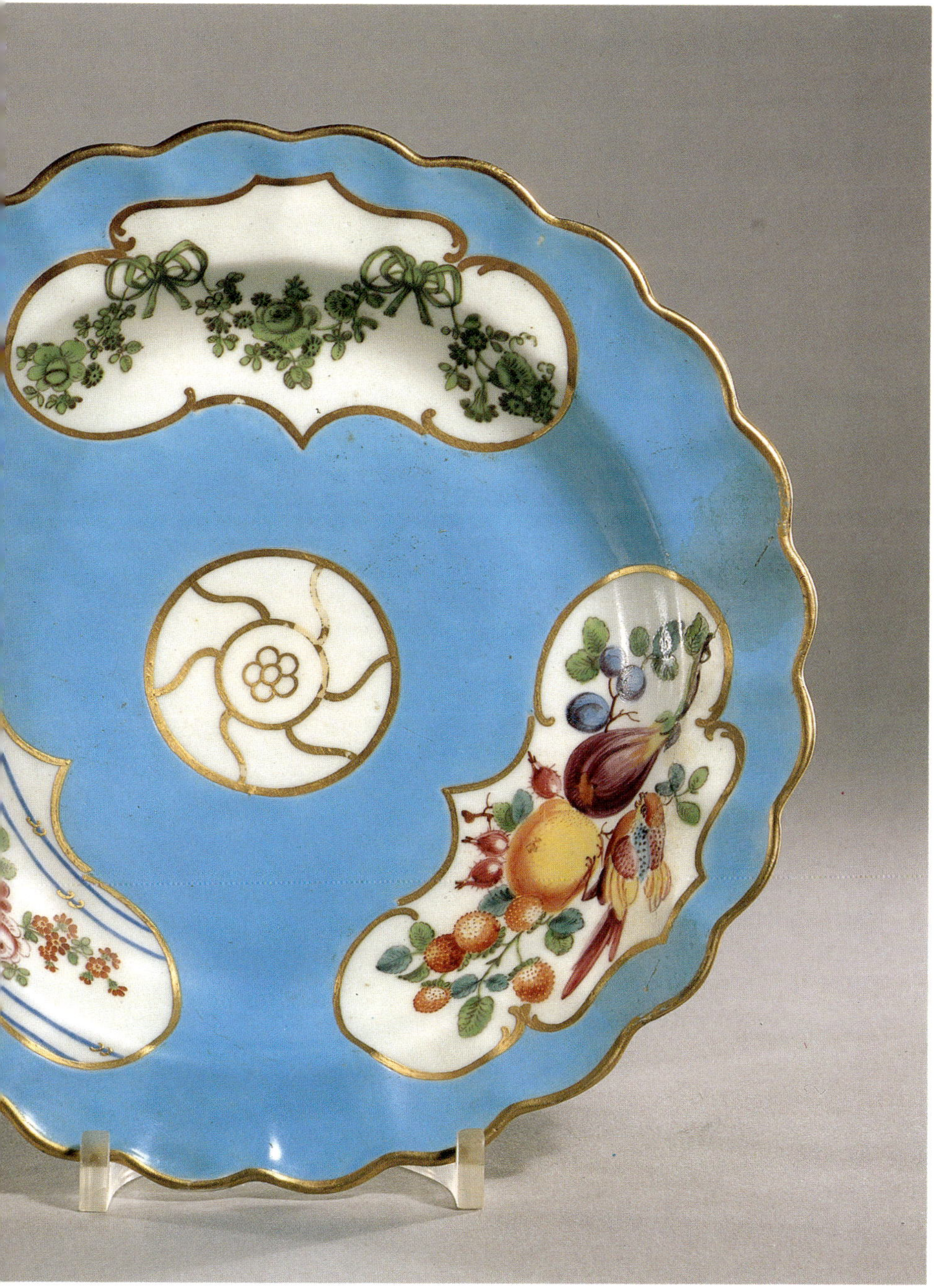

Plate 34

667–671 **Cabaret** circa 1770–72
Oval tray with wavy rim; barrel shaped teapot with flush cover and acorn finial; cylindrical sucrier with flat domed lid and acorn finial; ovoid milk jug; cup and saucer. Each piece decorated with 'dry' blue flower sprays and sprigs on a yellow ground. Gilt decoration on the handles. This decoration, consisting of chevrons diminishing in size, is often found on pieces decorated by James Giles.
It is extremely rare to find a complete cabaret. The name, which is French, refers to a tea or coffee set which has its own porcelain tray. If there is one cup it is a 'solitaire' and if two cups a 'tête à tête'.

Length of tray 30.5 cm. No mark.
Marshall, *op. cit.*, Plate 45, no. 927.
Jug exhibited Albert Amor, 1977, *op. cit.*, no. 75.
Tray illustrated Coke, *op. cit.*, Plate 54b.

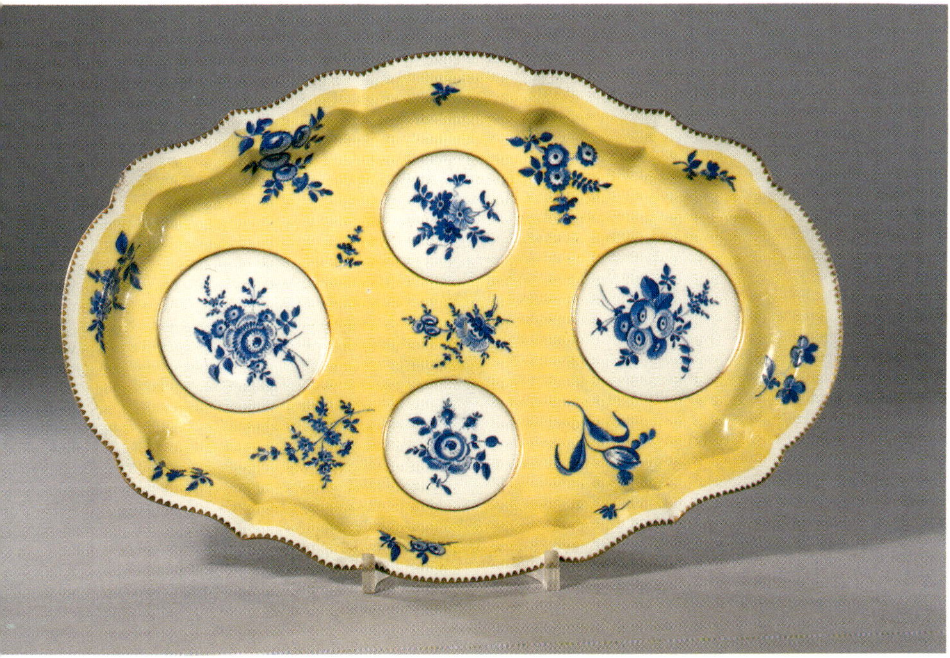

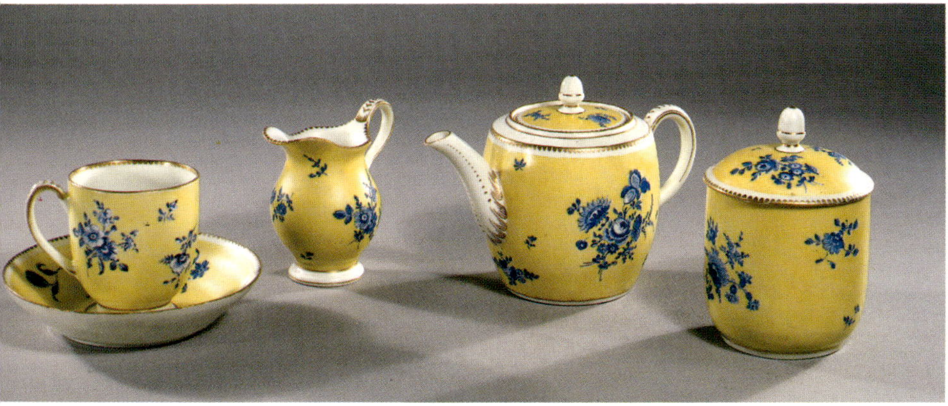

Plate 35

82 **Chestnut basket, cover and stand** circa 1770
of oval shape with quatrefoil outline. The cover and border of the stand are pierced and decorated with blue may flowers. The gilded branch handles of the basket terminate in encrusted flower sprays. The centre of the stand is painted with two angels and an exotic bird in a landscape.
This rare set was also decorated in the studio of James Giles. There are two other examples in the collection, nos. 413 and 434, which have red may flowers and brown handles.
Gerald Coke's book *In Search of James Giles* has extensive lists of patterns associated with the Giles atelier. The appendices include Giles's advertisements, ledger with the names of customers, and the 1774 sale catalogue. All these sources can help in deciding whether a piece was decorated in his London atelier or at the factory.

Length of stand 25.7 cm, height of basket and cover 12.7 cm. No mark.
Marshall, *op. cit.*, Plate 13, no. 229.
Stand exhibited Albert Amor, 1983, *op. cit.*, no. 55.

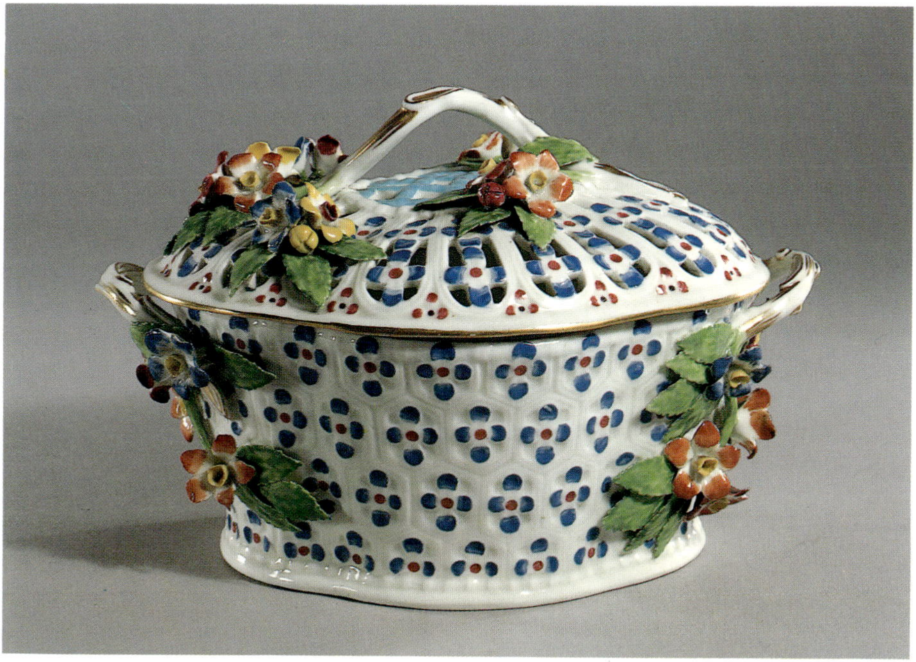

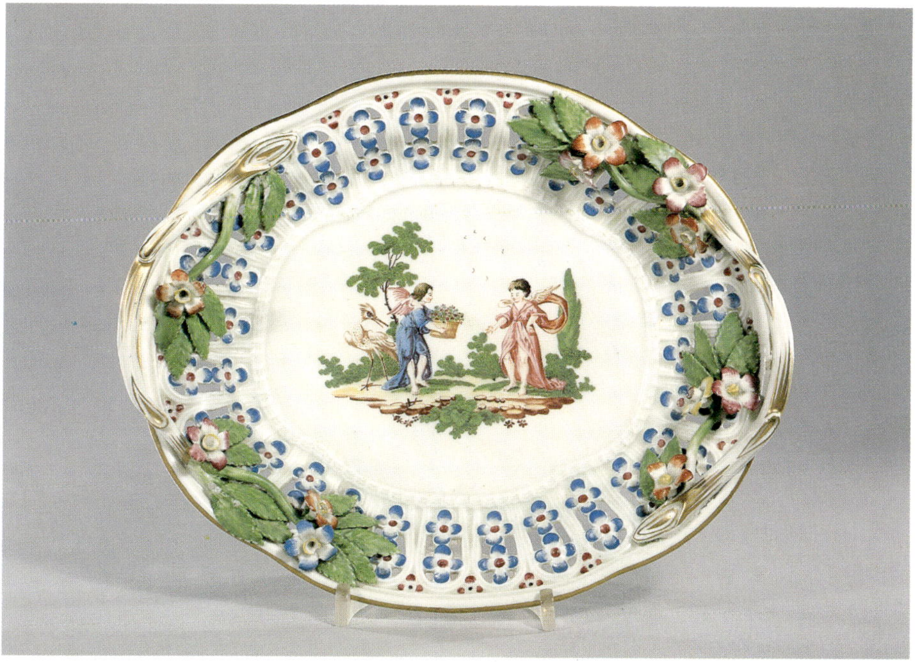

Select bibliography

H. R. Marshall, *Coloured Worcester Porcelain of the First Period* (1954).

F. A. Barrett, *Worcester Porcelain and Lund's Bristol* (1966).

H. Sandon, *Worcester Porcelain 1751–1793* (1980).

G. Coke, *In Search of James Giles* (1983).

S. Spero, *Worcester Porcelain: The Klepser Collection* (1984).

E. Leary & P. Walton, *Transfer-printed Worcester Porcelain at Manchester City Art Gallery* (n.d.).

Albert Amor catalogues:

1976 *Dr John Wall 1708–1776.*

1977 *James Giles, China Painter 1718–1780.*

1979 *Blue & White 18th Century Soft Paste Porcelain.*

1980 *The Golden Age. Masterpieces of 18th Century English Porcelain.*

1981 *Worcester Porcelain. The First Decade.*

1983 *The Elegant Porcelain of James Giles.*

1984 *The Wills Collection of Dr Wall Worcester Porcelain.*

1985 *The Sidders Collection of Dr Wall Worcester Porcelain.*

Acknowledgements

I would like to express my thanks to Mr Ian Lowe for introducing me to Worcester porcelain, to Mr Harry Frost, of the Dyson Perrins Museum, and Mr Simon Spero for their advice, but above all to Mrs Anne George, of Albert Amor Ltd, who gave uncomplainingly of her time and knowledge, and to my husband.

The photographs were all taken by Mr Michael Dudley in the Ashmolean studio, with the exception of the black and white photographs facing Plates 2 (courtesy Dyson Perrins Museum), 9, 19 and 33 (courtesy British Museum), and 30 (courtesy Victoria and Albert Museum).